KALEIDOSCOPE NOTES

ETHNOGRAPHIC ALTERNATIVES BOOK SERIES

Series Editors

Carolyn Ellis
Arthur P. Bochner
(both at the University of South Florida)

About the Series:

Ethnographic Alternatives emphasizes experimental forms of qualitative writing that blur the boundaries between social sciences and humanities.

The editors encourage submissions that experiment with novel forms of expressing lived experience, including literary, poetic, autobiographical, multi-voiced, conversational, critical, visual, performative, and co-constructed representations. Emphasis should be on expressing concrete lived experience through narrative modes of writing.

We are interested in ethnographic alternatives that promote narration of local stories; literary modes of descriptive scene setting, dialogue, and unfolding action; and inclusion of the author's subjective reactions, involvement in the research process, and strategies for practicing reflexive fieldwork.

Please send proposals to:

Carolyn Ellis and Arthur P. Bochner
College of Arts and Sciences
Department of Communication
University of South Florida
4202 East Fowler Avenue, CIS 1040
Tampa, FL 33620-7800
e-mail: cellis@chuma.cas.usf.edu

Books in the series:

Volume 1, *Composing Ethnography: Alternative Forms of Qualitative Writing*, Carolyn Ellis and Arthur P. Bochner, editors

Volume 2, *Opportunity House: Ethnographic Stories of Mental Retardation*, Michael V. Angrosino

Volume 3, *Kaleidoscope Notes: Writing Women's Music and Organizational Culture*, Stacy Holman Jones

KALEIDOSCOPE NOTES

Writing Women's Music and Organizational Culture

Stacy Holman Jones

ALTAMIRA
PRESS

A Division of Sage Publications, Inc.
Walnut Creek ▪ London ▪ New Delhi

For information address:

AltaMira Press
A Division of Sage Publications, Inc.
1630 North Main Street, Suite 367
Walnut Creek, CA 94596
explore@altamira.sagepub.com
http://www.altamirapress.com

SAGE Publications Ltd.
6 Bonhill Street
London EC2A 4PU
United Kingdom

SAGE Publications India Pvt. Ltd.
M-32 Market
Greater Kailash 1
New Delhi 110 048
India

PRINTED IN THE UNITED STATES OF AMERICA

Library of Congress Cataloging-in-Publication Data

Jones, Stacy Holman, 1966–
Kaleidoscope notes : writing women's music and organizational culture / Stacy Holman Jones.
  p. cm. — (Ethnographic alternatives book series; vol. 3)
  Includes bibliographical references and index.
  ISBN 0-7619-8965-X. — ISBN 0-7619-8966-8 (pbk.)
  1. Feminist music—Performances—California—San Francisco. 2. Lesbian music—Performances—California—San Francisco. 3. Club (San Francisco, Calif.) 4. Music-halls (Variety-theaters, cabarets, etc.)—California—San Francisco. 5. Corporate culture—California—San Francisco. I. Title. II. Series: Ethnographic alternatives book series; v. 3.
  ML82.J66 1998
  780'.82—dc21   97-45462
          CIP

Lyrics for "Ain't I A Woman," by Rory Block and Vinnie Martucci, and for "Road To Mexico" and "Mama's Blues," by Rory Block, ©1991 and 1992 by Happy Valley Music & Brown Foot Publishing. All rights reserved, used by permission.

Lyrics for "Act of Nature" and "75 Septembers," by Cheryl Wheeler, ©1993 by ACF Music, Penrod and Higgins Music/Amachrist Music. All rights reserved, used by permission.

Lyrics for "Getting It Right" and "Song of Myself," by Peggy Seeger, ©1973, 1972, and 1993. All rights reserved, used by permission.

Lyrics for "I'm Gonna Be an Engineer," by Peggy Seeger, ©1976 and 1979 by STORMKING MUSIC, INC. All rights reserved, used by permission.

With the exception of William F. (Bill) Owen, Sally J. Perkins, Gerri L. Smith, Nick Trujillo, and Cheryl Wheeler, all names, locations, and identities represented in this work have been disguised.

Contents

Dedication

IN MEMORY OF my grandfather John W. Blackburn, who taught me to hear the music in stories.

Series Editors' Introduction

ETHNOGRAPHIC ALTERNATIVES publishes experimental forms of qualitative writing that blur boundaries between social sciences and humanities. Books in this series feature concrete details of everyday life. People are presented as complicated and vulnerable human beings who act and feel in complex, often unpredictable ways. As social agents, constrained but not controlled by culture, they live stories that often show the dazzling human capacity to remake and reform cultural narratives.

We encourage authors in this series to write ethnography reflexively, weaving details about their own lives and relationships into the stories they tell about Others. Often authors seek to share interpretive authority by presenting layered accounts with multiple voices and by experimenting with nontraditional forms of representation, including the fictional and the poetic. They try to stay open to surprise and to encourage challenges and revisions to their own interpretations. In these books, interpretive authority ultimately rests with the community of readers who engage the text. When they are successful, these texts invite readers to feel, think about, and compare their own worlds of experience with those of the people they meet in these stories. In addition to contributing to conversation among academics across disciplinary lines, the books in the series are written in a fashion that makes them accessible to a wider audience, including people who can influence policy and social change.

In *Kaleidoscope Notes: Writing Women's Music and Organizational Culture*, Stacy Holman Jones writes and performs a kaleidoscope of conversation, fieldnotes, songs, interviews, poetry, stories, theories, and reflections on the meaning and experience of women's music, organizational culture, and ethnographic practices. She takes readers into the culture of The Club, a small, nonprofit, nonmainstream folk music venue, where employees and owners negotiate various musical, organizational, social, and political interests and challenges, yet still manage to persist and stay afloat. In The Club, she focuses on "women's music," which is music created and performed by women that depicts, embodies, and performs women as strong and persistent, music that problematizes relationships between gender identity and gender performance. Throughout, she reveals herself as an ethnographic actor, constantly challenging her own authority as author and attempting to collaborate with those she studies. She questions ethnographic practices, staging her thesis defense of this project as her final performance, where she plays to a full house consisting of her thesis committee; characters named Reliability, Validity, and their cousins, Voluptuous, Ironic, Paralogical, and Rhizomatic Validity; as well as reviewers and readers of this text.

Stacy Holman Jones encourages readers to experience bodily, aurally, and emotionally the mystery and magic of this organization, these musicians and their music, ethnographic method, and feminist and postmodern theory. Her work engages us as performers and as audience. She provokes us to compare and experience the tensions in The Club, in women's music, and in her struggle to find a space between resisting and accepting conventions in ethnographic writing practices where she can produce work that is intellectually honest and creative, yet socially approved and acceptable. The result is an open, provocative, and feminist text that performs, moves, changes, challenges, questions, reveals, and acts back on itself, blurring and bringing together truth and fiction, author and performer, audience and readers.

Carolyn Ellis and Arthur P. Bochner

Acknowledgments

O body swayed to music, o quickening glance,
How shall I tell the dancer from the dance?
W. B. Yeats, "Among School Children"

ACKNOWLEDGING everyone who assisted me in writing *Kaleidoscope Notes* is an impossible task. I am particularly indebted to:

Nick Trujillo for encouraging me at every turn

Carolyn Ellis and Art Bochner for believing in the power of stories

Joni Jones for making me feel at home in a new place

Don Jones for innumerable things

I greatly appreciate the support and enthusiasm of my family, Dean and Mary Holman; Jodi, Mark, and Sydnie Everette; and Bernice Holman, along with the Jones clan—many voices and many hearts.

I am grateful and blessed to know so many talented teachers and friends, particularly Gerri Smith, Sally Perkins, Mark Stoner, Bill Owen, Paul Gray, Lynn Miller, Georgine Hodgkinson, Eric Norton, Brenna Curtis, Rona Halualani, ReRe Pride, and Deanna Shoemaker, along with my esteemed instructors and colleagues at California State University, Sacramento and the University of Texas at Austin.

And there are others. Many thanks to Jennifer Collier and Mitch Allen at AltaMira and to Laurel Richardson for their tough questions and encouragement. And my sincere appreciation to the women's music artists whose music touched and shaped this work at every turn.

And, of course, I must thank the people of The Club for their dedication, for their feisty resolve . . . for their persistence.

Music is "a kaleidoscope of corners, each one reflecting the other, but also ensuring that the whole remains a multiplicity of parts."

Ann Powers, "Who's That Girl?"

As long as she writes little notes nobody objects to a woman writing.

Virginia Woolf, *Orlando*

Now, women forget all those things they don't want to remember, and remember everything they don't want to forget. The dream is the truth.

Zora Neale Hurston, *Their Eyes Were Watching God*

Authors/Notes

Dear Stacy:
My senses are stimulated
As I read this piece.
I keep asking about your
Intentions. Blurring, constructing,
Provoking. . . .

Leaving unspoken
Words about
Fact and fiction and self and
Other and participant and observer
And objectivity and
Infatuation.

Tell us.
Where does this project fit
Into the current landscape?
Into where ethnography lives,
And breathes,
Just now?

Don't leave us guessing.
Just talk to the reader.
Tell us what you feel.
Invite us
Into your experience.
Joni

Dear Joni . . . Dear reader:
This book is about
The spaces where
Fact and fiction collide
In a kaleidoscope of memory
And desire.

Text, music, self, other:
Endless rhythms, little notes,
Woven in culture.
Ethnographic truths,
Always partial, always
Wanting.

Still breathing in me,
Changing, moving.
Mine but not mine, alone.
Fashioned in the pulse
of experience, imagination
In tension.

Beginning at the end,
I remember everything
I don't want to forget.
I've learned to know more
And doubt that.
Now. . . .

With questioning embrace
Come dance inside this story.
Write novel truths, sing other
      voices,
It is your dream,
Your truth.

Music is 'a kaleidoscope of corners, each one reflecting the other, but also ensuring that the whole remains a multiplicity of parts.'

Ann Powers, "Who's That Girl?"[1]

I like the feeling there. It's a safe place where you can listen to the music, enjoy yourself. It's just a real easy place to be.

Sharon, night manager of The Club

We are 'walking contradictions, partly truth and partly fiction.' The challenge for women writing culture is to grasp the truth value of our contradictions.

Janet L. Finn, "Ella Cara Deloria and Mourning Dove"[2]

1

Mother's Music

I AM WAITING.

The graduate faculty look down on me from glass and chrome frames, their smiles hard and distant in the shadowy display case. I pace back and forth along the row of photos, then stop and stare into the eyes of Gerri, Nick, and Bill, my thesis committee. It's been more than twenty minutes since they asked me to wait in the hallway outside the conference room. I search their faces for a sign, for some insight to what they're thinking and saying about my work—about *me*. Laughter builds low inside the room and rushes to where I stand. What are they *laughing* about? The door jerks open.

"Stacy?" Gerri calls. "We're ready for you."

What had taken so long? Why the formality of asking me to leave the room? Other students' prospectus defenses had been brief, almost relaxed. I shrug off a twinge of panic and turn the corner into the hallway. When I slide into the chair across from them, Nick and Bill smile at me.

"We think this is an exciting project," Gerri begins. I exhale, realizing I'd been holding my breath.

She smiles. "Your proposal makes a clear case for studying the culture of a music-oriented organization, and your decision to pursue ethnographic methods is appropriate. However, we have some issues we want you to consider before beginning your fieldwork."

"My main concern," Nick interjects, "is your oscillation between interpretive and critical theory. Do you intend on doing a critical ethnography?"

My heart begins to race. "I'm not sure. . . ."

"You need to decide. And we'll need to come up with some solid criteria for judging the thesis once it's written."

My palms begin to sweat. "Criteria?"

"Yes. We must be able to assess whether you've met the goals laid out in the prospectus. And because you've chosen to experiment with writing style and form, these criteria are especially important."

"Well," I begin, "the text needs to be evocative. It must create the field experience—make the field come alive for the reader. And it should communicate the experience of the researcher."

"That's a start," Nick interrupts. "But you need to understand. This kind of work has traditionally been subject to much criticism. It cannot be seen as some kind of easy or evasive alternative to social science. . . ."

This time I interrupt. "I don't think what I want to accomplish is easy or evasive. . . ."

"Neither do we," Nick says, "but as graduate faculty and members of your committee, we have a responsibility to push you to identify what constitutes a rigorous and legitimate alternative ethnographic text. A responsibility to ensure that you defend your work according to those criteria."

"This doesn't have to be decided today," Gerri adds. "But we want you to begin thinking about it. And, of course, we'll help you with these decisions."

"OK," I say, eager to have this meeting over, to escape the tight air of the room. "I'll put something together for you to review."

"That's fine with me," Gerri says. "Nick, Bill?"

Nick and Bill nod.

"Everything else seems to be in order," Gerri continues. "Your interview schedule looks good, you've identified an appropriate number of individuals to speak with, and the observations you've planned should prove useful. I think we're ready to sign."

"One last question," Bill says, startling me. He's been silent most of the meeting. "Why study The Club? Why this organization?"

"*What?*" a voice deep inside screams. Hadn't I at least made that clear?

"Yeah," Nick interjects. "Why not study the Grateful Dead as you'd planned?"

"It seems like you could do this study just about anywhere," Bill adds.

"As I explained in my proposal," I begin, then stop, surprised by a sudden sting of tears. I swallow hard, push down the emotion. "I don't think I can explain it any better than I have in the proposal . . . it just feels right."

*   *   *

"Do you mind if I record our conversation?" I ask, shaky hands offering her a look at my mini-cassette recorder.

"That's fine," she says. She's taller than I'd imagined, with shiny gray hair and milky skin. Morning light streams through the windows and dances in her eyes.

"Great. If you're ready to get started. . . ."

"Sure."

"I'm here with Natalie Allen, founder and first owner of The Club," I say for the benefit of the recorder. "Natalie, can you tell me how The Club got its start?"

"It was really a happy accident. Let's see . . . it was 1968, and I was teaching in Oakland, but I knew I didn't want to teach. My uncle left me some money, so I quit and traveled around the country for six months. When I was in Greenwich Village, I fell in love with the coffeehouses there, with the whole scene. After I got back to the San Francisco Bay Area, I looked up a girlfriend who had some restaurant experience and we decided to do a coffeehouse."

"The Club?"

"Yeah. Our first location—you know we used to be on San Fernando Avenue?"

"Yes."

"Right. So we rented the building on San Fernando. We built a small kitchen, opened the doors, and people started coming. It wasn't the Ritz, but we gave it a homey feeling. The rest is history."

"Do you remember the first night you were open?"

"Oh yes, Take Me to Heaven, an old-timey folk band, played. The fiddle player was a friend who'd called and asked for the first booking. From the start, musicians just called up or came by and asked to play."

"How about the audiences? Did you do much advertising?"

Natalie laughs, beaded earrings brushing her shoulders. "We were too broke for advertising. It was a pretty small community back then. People would come to hear their friends play on Friday, then be on stage Saturday."

"What kind of music did you do?"

"Mostly folk, country, bluegrass. But we'd also have jazz, blues, even some world music. Lots of singer-songwriters."

"Did you have hoot nights back then?"

"Sure. That's a tradition we started. Every Tuesday night was hoot night."

"Can you tell me about it?"

"It's a night when new performers can come and play for an audience, get advice and some much-needed stage experience. Some great players got their start at The Club's hoots."

"Such as?"

"Oh, people like Allison Krauss and Shawn Colvin."

"I saw Shawn Colvin on television last week."

Natalie smiles proudly. "Hoot night has become a tradition in this community."

"When did you begin publishing the calendar?"

"That started early on. We'd established our weekly routine—hoot nights on Tuesdays, music Wednesdays through Sundays, closed Mondays. It just made sense to put out a monthly calendar. Two high school students who hung out at The Club started doing the illustrations."

"I've heard the early calendars have become collector's items."

"I'm sure they have." Natalie looks into her coffee mug and smiles.

"So tell me about The Club crowd in those early years," I say, anxious to understand that smile.

"Well, as I said, a good number were musicians. Mostly locals, not many college students since we were a good bit from the university. Young, old, male, female . . . people from all sorts of ethnic groups. A real eclectic crowd."

"Have things changed?"

"When we started, folk music, and even bluegrass to some extent, was enjoying a real resurgence. It was more mainstream than it is today. Today's Club caters to a very defined segment of the community. The kind of music they put on, which hasn't changed substantially from the early days, is real specific to that population. It's not mainstream any more."

"What role did politics play with the early artists and audiences?"

Her eyes widen. "Interesting question. I'd have to say that while politics were certainly part of why we were there, they were secondary to the music. We never booked artists because we agreed with their politics. We were more interested in the *music* . . . whether it was technically and artistically sound, inspirational, masterful."

"I didn't see a show at the San Fernando location, so I have a hard time imagining what attending a performance there must've felt like. Can you describe that for me?"

"Well, the audience was generally a listening bunch. It was always very quiet when the artists were playing. And there was no drinking. We had coffee and brownies and good music . . . an occasional game of chess."

"Sounds like things haven't changed much."

"I haven't been to The Club in a good bit."

"How come?"

"I've just sort of grown away from it. In some ways, it's difficult to be there."

"How so?"

She sighs. "As much as I loved it, The Club took an enormous amount of time and energy to run. We never really made a profit— although that's not what we were after—but there were months when we could barely keep the doors open. We didn't have money for a payroll. My salary was fifty dollars a week when we could afford it. Everyone else volunteered. . . . More than once artists played by candlelight because we couldn't pay the light bill. And people played for free. After ten years of that kind of uncertainty, I was tired and ready to get out."

"So you sold The Club."

Natalie nods slowly. "Yes. I sold it to a friend, Leah Halsey. Not long after that, Leah sold The Club to a couple who ran it until they went nonprofit sometime during the '80s."

" '83, I think."

"That sounds right," she says.

"What have you been doing since you sold The Club?"

"I got into physical therapy."

"You enjoy that?"

"Yes, very much. . . . In a way, it feels like an extension of what I did at The Club—healing people, providing a place for them to find their wings. . . ."

She is silent. I wait.

"Even though I haven't been there for five or six years, there's not a day goes by I don't think about those times . . . that I'm not glad there were dedicated people who made sure The Club survived."

"All because of your efforts."

"Not just mine," she corrects. "The Club was always about much more than personal effort. It was about people coming together and working for something they believed in. . . ." Natalie takes a long sip from her mug. She closes her eyes as she swallows.

"I have one last question," I say.

"Sure."

"You started The Club at a time when women were struggling for equal rights, fighting for political and social freedom. How important was it to have women play a significant role in this organization? Was that part of your agenda?"

"Hmm." She removes wire-framed glasses and rubs her eyes. "Right from the start, women played an enormous role in what we were doing. In fact, up until Leah sold The Club, it was operated solely by women. . . . I don't know I would say it was part of our agenda, more than it just worked out that way. And women have always performed there, have always brought something special to the stage."

"How so?"

"Just by being good at what they do. By showing the kinds of contributions women can make through their music."

"Were they women's music artists?"

"I was never sure what that term meant."

"I'm trying to get a handle on it myself. I think it's music that focuses on women's experience. Music that makes a political statement about being a woman in the world."

Natalie nods. "I guess some of the early performers could be counted among women's music artists. Some couldn't. They were all women *musicians*. Do you know what I mean?"

"I think so."

"Our primary goal was to create a nurturing and safe environment for the artists, and for the people who came to hear the music. Whether that's a feminist goal, I don't know. But we did create that kind of environment. It's one of the things I'm most proud of."

* * *

Natalie offers to make us some tea. I settle back into the couch and listen to the sounds of glass and water. A conversation I'd had with Gerri in her office a few days before begins to play in my head. Anxious about my first interview, I'd stopped by for a little encouragement. Gerri motioned for me to enter her office. "Hey," she said into the telephone, "I've got to go. I have a student." She finished the call, then turned her gaze on me. "How's the fieldwork coming?"

"OK. I've got an interview with the founder this weekend. I think she'll give me some good stuff."

"Good. Not as glamorous as the Grateful Dead, though," she said, then smiled.

"It was a half-baked idea two years ago. Maybe Nick should do that study. This just seems much more important. At least to me."

"Then it is," Gerri said. "It is."

*   *   *

"It is," I say quietly.

"Pardon me?" Natalie asks, interrupting my thoughts. She places the tea on the coffee table next to my forgotten tape recorder.

"Oh, um, I enjoyed hearing your thoughts," I say and reach for the recorder. "Thanks."

"Enough ancient history," she says and smiles. "Why don't you tell me about the first time *you* went to The Club. What intrigued you?"

"It must have been about two years ago. My husband, Don, and I were visiting his sister and we decided to go out and hear some music. When we pulled up in front of The Club, I wasn't sure whether going there was such a good idea."

Natalie laughs. "A pretty homely façade, huh?"

"I thought we'd be mugged! My brother-in-law, Steve, said, 'This place is a Bay Area institution.' It sure looked like one. When he pried open that massive wooden door, we all rushed inside."

"An equally impressive sight."

"Yeah, but it just looks thrown together, not menacing."

"They've been accumulating those chairs since I was around."

"It certainly felt like a nonprofit. Cramped space. Peeling paint."

"And the crowd?"

"Mostly white and middle-aged, except for a few small children, a couple of college students, a group of Asian women. And the smell of coffee was so strong. It hung over us like a fog."

"That's what I remember most about The Club. The coffee smell. It sticks to you. What did you think of the music?"

"When the music started, I was surprised. We saw Grant Brown. Do you know him?"

"Name sounds familiar. What was the music like?"

"A mix of folk and blues. He was a wonderful player and very funny. And the audience was incredibly attentive—a listening bunch, as you put it. They sat so straight in those unforgiving chairs, almost meditating on the performance. And I felt how music communicates something words alone can't."

Natalie nods. "It's a sensuous kind of communication."

"Yes. It creates a powerful, almost mysterious feeling of communion."

"Music can do that. Is that why you chose The Club as the focus of your project?"

"Not initially. I chose The Club because I was interested in studying the culture of a nonprofit organization. Music was an interest for me, but I wasn't sure how to get at the intangible feelings *I* had about music within a study of organizational culture. Not sure, at least, until I went to that first performance at The Club."

Natalie closes her eyes. A serene smile plays on her lips. "And you knew."

"Yes. At least I knew I had to try. And I knew I wanted to do an ethnography."

"An ethnography?"

I laugh. "Sounds painfully official, huh? It's just what we've been talking about—asking questions about what experience means to us—now and over time."[3]

The corners of Natalie's lips inch upward, teasing her smile into a grin. "How do you ask questions about the meaning of The Club experience?"

"That's the real challenge! Of course, I had to come up with a research question to get the go-ahead to do the study, but it's so general it's not much use. . . ."

"I'd like to hear it."

I clear my throat and feel a twinge of embarrassment about the academic righteousness of the words I'm about to speak. " 'How is the culture—the essence of The Club as an organization—expressed in the performances staged there?' It sounds sterile, I know, but. . . ."

"No," Natalie says. "It's an interesting question. Now . . . how do you propose to answer it?"

"Well . . . by observing and participating and writing about The Club. Truth is, I'm not entirely sure how I'll go about discovering the meaning of The Club experience. Or about what I'll find."

Smiling, she says, "Remember, the joy is in the journey."

*   *   *

I stand in the middle of The Club, empty except for the tangle of folding chairs clustered around tiny Formica tables. I turn, slowly, trying to memorize every detail—white Christmas lights clinging to onyx walls, coarse wooden sign, faded Kilim rug covering the stage. I record these facts in my notebook, uncertain what they reveal about The Club or the ethnographer. I'm eager to write, to *possess* this space, as if understanding the stretch and quiet of The Club will help me grasp the magic of what happens here.

Turning again, I hear whispers of guitar and piano. I feel the heat of applause and candlelight. These are the things I want to know, the things I can't see or write. I want to feel the artistry, the reverence, the fire of this place. I want to love it as they do, but I'm not sure how to get inside. And then I remember . . . it was the music that brought me here.

Notes

1. Ann Powers, "Who's That Girl?," *Rock She Wrote: Women Write About Rock, Pop, and Rap,* ed. Evelyn McDonnell and Ann Powers (New York: Delta, 1995), 462.
2. Janet L. Finn, "Ella Cara Deloria and Mourning Dove: Writing for Cultures, Writing Against the Grain," *Women Writing Culture,* ed. Ruth Behar and Deborah A. Gordon (Berkeley: University of California Press, 1995), 144.
3. Renato Rosaldo, *Culture and Truth: The Remaking of Social Analysis* (Boston: Beacon Press, 1993), 37. The author writes, "The once-dominant ideal of a detached observer using neutral language to explain 'raw' data has been displaced by an alternative project that attempts to understand human conduct as it unfolds through time and in relation to its meanings for the actors."

... The torment that so many young women know, bound hand and foot by love and motherhood without having forgotten their former dreams.

Simone de Beauvior, *All Said and Done*[1]

When the band was setting up for a showcase arranged for label executives who were visiting from London, I noticed someone pointing to a monitor directly in front of me and telling a technician to move it 'so the pigs can see her legs.'

Margot Mifflin, "The Fallacy of Feminism in Rock"[2]

Sound's great, but she's got this massive monitor and we can't see her play. And I'm staring right at her crotch.

Male patron of The Club

Fiction reveals truths reality obscures.

Jessamyn West, quoted in *The Quotable Woman*[3]

2

Ain't I a Woman?

"SO WHERE *ARE* YOU?" Josh stammers. Lina glances at her watch. She'd forgotten Josh was working nights at the lab. She'd called too early.

"Sorry, hon. Forgot you're on nights. I'm at The Club. We're doing shows here tonight and Friday."

"Then you're headed home?"

"Yeah, baby, then home. This tour's been hell. You get your projects done?"

"Mom, you sound exhausted. Your voice is shot."

"It'll make it. So tell me. Am I the exhausted mother of a college graduate?"

"Whadaya think?"

"I got Colleen working on getting me there. Ten o'clock, right?"

"Mom. I don't want you killing yourself to get here. I don't even want to go to the ceremony."

"This isn't for you, it's for me. I want to see you walk across that stage."

"I'll be there. *You* just show up."

The dressing room door creaks, opens slowly. Jerry Wells, Lina's manager, pokes his head in.

"OK, babe. Hey, I gotta go. Jerry's here."

"You tell that manager of yours to stop working you so hard."

Lina chuckles. "OK. Love you, Josh."

"You too. See you Saturday."

Lina returns the receiver to its cradle. She bows her head and runs her fingers through her hair. Raising her chin, she meets Jerry's eyes.

"Hey J. How many tonight?"

"Gonna have a great crowd. Two hundred tonight, two-fifty tomorrow."

Lina considers Jerry as he pats the pockets of his jacket searching for cigarettes. Lina has known Jerry since they were kids. He used to tag along with his uncle and play banjo in her Poppy's jam sessions. His picking talent is legendary, but he'd quit the music business fifteen years ago; said he was tired of all the traveling and cheap motels.

Jerry and Lina have had their share of ups and downs. Seems as if every few years or so, loneliness would drive them together, her restlessness always making sure their affairs never lasted long. A couple of years ago, Jerry said he couldn't see Lina anymore, couldn't take her occasional affection. He'd agreed to manage this year's tour only after some serious pleading, and he's made the exhausting trip almost enjoyable—politely hassling with bookings and hotel managers, playing cribbage until dawn when Lina can't sleep—but the strain of all these months on the road has crept into his smile, his eyes.

"Hope the crowd's got enough energy to keep me going tonight. I'm dead. I can't do this shit anymore," Lina says.

"Only two more, honey," Jerry mutters, then slips out the door.

*   *   *

Subj: Ethno
Date: 22 Oct. 1995
From: nickt@csus.edu
To: stacyhj@aol.com

Hey, how's the ethnography coming?

I stare at the computer screen and feel an aching pang of responsibility. The ethnography isn't coming, or going, anywhere. For weeks I've been stuck and I'm embarrassed to talk about it. The writing isn't progressing and my research just seems like an endless trip through a revolving door. Just when I think I'm on to something—about to step out into a wide, open room—a new book or article pulls me back into the vestibule and around again. The frustrating thing is, the more time I spend at The Club, the more I feel a driving need to understand it. The question is, how do I write about it? I maneuver the mouse to the top of the computer screen, then click "reply."

Subj: Ethno
Date: 23 Oct. 1995
From: stacyhj@aol.com
To: nickt@csus.edu

Nick: The ethnography is stuck at the moment. I'm drowning in a sea of fieldnotes, theory, interviews, and methods texts. Not sure where one ends and the next begins. Also, the term "women's music" has come up in several interviews and I'm not sure how to characterize it. What if I looked strictly at "women's music" performances? Might be a way to give some focus to my work. What do you think? Stacy

The next afternoon, I watch the clock, wishing I could put away my reading and set out on the two-hour drive to The Club to see Lina Michaels—a women's music performer who'd come highly recommended. Stalling, I check my e-mail for the fifth time that day, hoping Nick has sent a reply. He has.

. . . .

Subj: Ethno
Date: 24 Oct. 1995
From: nickt@csus.edu
To: stacyhj@aol.com

The "women's music" angle sounds good. Be sure you get a handle on what that genre is all about. And don't lose sight of the story. Write the *story.*

. . . .

*   *   *

Sharon pokes her head around the dressing room door to get a glimpse of the crowd. The room is steadily filling. She sees Gwen and Danny Silva in the front row. They're beaming with delight from the seats she'd saved for them.

"Sharon, you're an angel," Danny had cooed when she led them to the front row.

"You've been waiting for Lina's tour to swing through here since last March," she reminded him. "This is a special night."

"We're a bit envious, you getting to see *both* of Lina's shows," Gwen teased. "Do you catch much when you're working?"

"I used to when I worked the counter," Sharon said. "Since I've become a night manager, I'm here so much I've sort of gotten my fill of music. I rarely turn on my stereo or listen to the car radio anymore. Most nights here I listen to the first set, then hole up in the office to count the door cash and get the musicians' pay together."

"Hmm," Danny interrupted in a puff of surprise. "I wonder if I'd ever get anything done with distractions like Lina around."

"Tonight will be different," Sharon agreed. "I'll wait 'til the last minute to get my work done so I can catch Lina's performance."

Now it's time to start the show. Sharon climbs the two tall steps leading to the stage and steps lightly to the microphone. Shoving her hands into the front pockets of her jeans, she smiles out at the crowd.

"Good evening," she whispers into the microphone, then clears her throat. "Good evening," she booms, laughing. The flame of conversation among the crowd flickers and dies out. Anxious eyes settle on her.

"Welcome to The Club. How many of you are new here?" Porcelain hands sprout up from the vibrant mass of curls, knit caps, and scarves.

"For those of you who are new, and for those of you who don't know," Sharon says, squinting into the spotlight, "The Club is a non-profit organization dedicated to bringing the best in traditional music to the Bay Area. And we've been doing just that since 1968. Some of the great sounds we've got planned for October include bluegrass with Wendy Wilson and the Big Blue Band on the 5th, the hard-driving Celtic energy of Steeped in Fire on the 26th, and the much-awaited pairing of Cher Wilson and Tracy Firey on November 2nd." A whisper of anticipation ripples through the crowd.

"Tickets for all these shows are on sale now. If you're planning on catching the Wilson–Firey show, buy your tickets early. It's a guaranteed sell-out." Sharon shoves the sleeves of her sweater toward her elbows. Beads of perspiration freckle her forehead and cheeks.

"OK, just one more announcement. There are recycling bins near the concession counter in the front near the restrooms. Please recycle your glass and cans."

Sharon pauses, then smiles. "I'm pleased to introduce Majestic recording artist Lina Michaels." She reaches for the bulky half-glasses tethered around her neck and unfolds a crumpled page smeared with her handwriting. "A student of legendary bluesmen Slim Smith and Martin Segals, Lina's fierce playing and vocals reflect the tutelage of these great players. Her latest album, *The Woman has the Blues*, is chock full of searing women's blues tunes. Of her latest, *Folk Sounds* critic Billy Morgan writes, 'Lina has handpicked an intense set of blues cuts, all laced with great acoustic guitar artistry and laden with universal emotions of the human condition'." Sharon tugs at the glasses and lets them fall to her chest.

"Let's give a big welcome to Lina Michaels." She begins a thunder of applause. Lina slips from the dressing room and up the stairs to the stage. As Sharon retreats, Lina takes her place in front of the microphone. She clasps her hands in front of her and basks in the glow of applause.

*   *   *

I record snippets of Sharon's introduction in my notebook, straining in the dim light to see my writing seep onto the page. "Searing women's blues . . . universal emotions/human condition . . . what makes this 'women's' blues? Why not just blues? Lina is tall, dark, powerful."

Feeling self-conscious, I stop writing and cover the notebook with my hands, then settle back against the chair. Lina begins and her voice envelops the room. My heart pounds in my ears. "A great ethnography night," I write as if I might forget how this feels. It doesn't happen on every visit, these nights when my hands go cold, my chest tightens in anticipation of something out of the ordinary, some striking insight.

The feeling reminds me of interviews I conducted with Club employees and performers, and with members of its board of directors. To relax the conversation, I'd ask people to tell me stories. "Tell me about times you've been to The Club and felt that something special was going on there," I'd say and wait until a smile burst across their faces. It always happened. They'd say, "The air was electric," and "There was a sense of magic," and "I'm glad I was there because I thought this may never happen again," and "It's hard to talk about."

This mysterious feeling, about music and about ethnography, was what drew me to The Club, not the study of organizational culture, not a thesis.

Sitting in the audience, I want to explain the mystery. I want to *capture* it, but I'm not sure how. "Writing seems so far away," I scribble without looking at the page, then push the incapable notebook into my jacket.

*　　*　　*

Lina squints at her set list and reads "Road To M." She begins to tune her guitar, then drops her hands, letting the instrument hang in front of her.

"Colleen?" she calls, shielding her eyes from the stage lights and searching the crowd. "Can you check the bass?" She touches her face with a lace-trimmed towel.

"I'm having trouble getting the sound right," Lina explains to eager eyes. "I'll do 'Ain't I A Woman' for you while I still have my voice, then take a break and we'll see if we can't get this fixed."

She turns away from the audience and places her guitar in the stand next to her chair, then stands and pulls the microphone from its grip.

"I wrote this song after I read Sojourner Truth's speech of the same title. Sojourner said, 'That man over there say that woman needs to be helped into carriages and lifted over ditches, and have the best place everywhere. Nobody ever helps me into carriages, or over mud puddles. And ain't I a woman?' " Lina gathers inky black hair in handfuls, then lets it cascade down her back. She moves to the edge of the stage, pulling us into her story.

"Sojourner Truth had thirteen children, and she watched most of them sold into slavery and die. When I heard her words . . . words that were as moving as those spoken by any of the great speakers of her time, I cried. I cried because this simple woman, an uneducated woman, understood the injustice of her life. She spoke of the plight of African Americans and also of women.

"So I wrote this song. The first verse is a paraphrase of her speech. The second, third, and fourth verses are about women, but they are also about many, many people." Lina takes a breath and pierces the quiet with her voice. She draws the melody from deep within, thrusting energy and anger into the room.

*

*Sojourner Truth had 13 children, and each and every one was sold in
slavery,
She said I can work the fields, and carry water like a man,
I can do all these things she said.
And ain't I a woman?*

*I've been beaten and abandoned,
I've walked across this earth with no place to call my home,
I'll sing it in a song and tell it in a story, that I still am strong 'cause,
Ain't I a woman?*

*I live alone, my children are all gone,
I raised them up with no husband by my side,
One is gone to God, and two live in Georgia,
But I carry on 'cause.
Ain't I a woman?*

*They say let your light shine,
Let it so shine upon the world,
And your eyes behold the simple truth,
That my heart is filled with strong compassion
And this fire forever burns 'cause,
Ain't I a woman?*[4]

*

Lina closes her mouth, cutting off the sound and letting it float out
over the audience. The sudden surge of applause pushes her back on
her heels. Tears shine in the corners of her eyes, then spill over her
cheeks. She bows her head, then whirls in quick retreat. The heat of
their veneration rises and trails after her into the dressing room.

*   *   *

"Ain't I a woman," I write, trying to funnel the excitement I feel into
words. "Sojourner Truth. Also title of bell hooks' book.[5] Forceful,

touching song . . . certainly *this* is women's music? Though Lina says it's about many, many people. Is it about me? Ain't I a woman?"

*   *   *

"I'll get the sound straightened out," Colleen begins as soon as the dressing room door opens. "And I'm so sorry about the amp. I don't know how I could've left it behind. I called the . . ."

"Colleen, I told you not to worry about it," Lina says. "I just need you to get my guitar in tune and fix the bass. Where's J.?" She searches the contents of an expansive tapestry bag. "Do you have any cough drops?"

Lina looks up at Colleen, who is chewing her lower lip. "What's wrong?"

"Oh Lina," Colleen sobs. "I'm sorry. I've made such a mess of things."

"You're doing just fine. It gets this way at the end of a tour, with everyone tired and barely able to think straight. You've done wonders for me and J."

"You know how much I appreciate you taking me in," Colleen says, wiping her nose with her shirt sleeve. "I just wish I could do a better job for you. . . ."

"So young," Lina thinks as Colleen talks. "She's barely older than your own son, and you've got her taking care of the equipment and travel. . . . Well, *J*. has her taking care of it. And he's been so down these last months. Seems Colleen's the only person who can cheer him up."

"Colleen," Lina interrupts, offering a smile. "Keep working on that National I gave you, and someday I'll have you on stage playin' rhythm."

She pulls Colleen close, hugs her hard and quick, then pulls away to look into weepy brown eyes. "Until then, please, *please*, get my guitar in tune for the second set."

Colleen smiles and turns to leave the dressing room. As she reaches for the door, Lina calls out, "A Diet Coke on stage?"

"Sure, Lina."

"Thanks, honey. And if you see J., will you send him in?"

"Yeah."

"He's been acting pretty strange the last few days."

Colleen stops in the doorway, her back to Lina's words.

"Will you talk to him? See what's up?"

"Sure, Lina."

Colleen takes the stage to tune Lina's guitar, gently removing it from its cradle and bending her head toward the monitor to do her work quietly. Through her eyelashes, she sees a bearded man approach.

"Excuse me," the man says. "Is there any way you could move this monitor?"

Colleen looks at the large black box next to her ear, then at the man. "Uh, no," she stammers. "Lina needs it there so she can hear the guitar."

"Well, it's directly in our line of sight and we can't see her hands."

Colleen cringes, inhales. "That *is* a problem, but I can't move it. I'm sorry."

"We can't see her play," the bearded man persists. "We can only see her left hand."

Colleen clears her throat. "Sir, I *am* sorry," she explains. "This isn't our usual monitor. It's a loaner from The Club. We left ours in Portland last night. I understand your trouble, but I can't move it."

"We can't see her," he says, then pauses, mouth open. He turns and strides away. Colleen breathes a sigh of relief, then bows her head to the guitar.

*　　*　　*

I scribble in my notebook, trying to make sense of the exchange between the stage assistant and the man. "Stage assistant young, blonde. Man tall with thick, reddish beard. He's obviously upset, but what can she do?" I pause to consider the man's request. He's sitting in the front row, and he's obviously interested in watching Lina's guitar work. She is, after all, an artist, and he wants to observe her closely.

There's also something disturbing about his request. Is Lina under surveillance—her every move catalogued, evaluated by the audience? Isn't it enough to *hear* the music, to feel the strength and emotion in her songs? I make a note: "Does the man want access to her artistry? Does he need to see her create the music?" I stop and stare up at the ceiling, then return to the notebook. "Does he want to possess her talent, as Hunter says, because 'Women are always public' and 'always available for male intrusions,' their 'surveillance' a mechanism of male 'social control'?[6] Is bearded man exercising his *right* to surveillance and social control?"

My thoughts are interrupted by the stare of a man sitting a few seats away. I feel him watching me, looking at my notebook, my face, my body. I don't want to explain what I'm doing here, what I'm writing. Before he can ask the inevitable, "Are you taking notes?" I stand and walk toward the lobby.

I see the bearded man. He's talking with Bill, a regular I'd met a few weeks ago. Hoping for a hello and an opportunity to ask a few questions, I make my way toward their conversation.

*   *   *

"How's the record coming?" the bearded man asks Bill. "Are you ever gonna get that damn thing recorded?"

"It's getting there," Bill says. "Two more cuts, and we'll have it wrapped up."

"Great," the bearded man says. "So what do you think?"

"Lina? Ah, she's terrific. 'Joliet Bound'[7] was incredible. I'm surprised she didn't break all her strings on that one."

"Sharon got us seats in the front row tonight," he brags.

"S'that right?" Bill asks with a chuckle. "How's the sound from the expensive seats?"

"Sound's great, but she's got this massive monitor and we can't see her play. And I'm staring right at her crotch."

"Kind of distracting?" Bill says, then smiles.

He beams. "She's an attractive woman. Makes it hard to concentrate. She has pants on, though, so I'm OK."

"Don't have a heart attack," Bill teases, bringing his big hand down hard on the bearded man's shoulder. "I see your wife waiting on you. Better get back in there."

"Yeah," he says, distracted. "You take it easy."

*   *   *

"Bearded man talks to Bill about not being able to see Lina's hands," I scratch in my notebook as I plop into a seat in the back row of The Club. I write quickly to make sure I don't miss anything.

" 'She has pants on though, so I'm OK' . . . 'Don't have a heart attack' . . . Performer is under surveillance? A musician, yes, but a woman first? Does her sexuality distract from her performance? Her body is the *site* of performance . . . the text inhabits/becomes synonymous with the performer's body—a woman's body. Implies a relationship of struggle between performer, text, and audience borne out in visual surveillance.[8] Does the man focus on Lina's body, seeing it as an instrument for the text, rather than seeing her as a performer or seeing the performance itself? Is his discomfort with Lina as a person—as a woman? Does he want to see her only as an instrument for the music? What if Lina were a man?"

The lights blink on and off quickly once, then twice more. I look up from my notes, disoriented. Intermission is nearly over. I decide to buy a cup of coffee before the second set begins. I'll need it to stay awake on the long drive home.

*   *   *

"How's the door cash, Virginia?" asks Sharon. "I hope Lina's show makes up for the disappointing turnout for the Balkan choral group last night."

"Sold nearly fifty tickets at the door. Twenty or so standing-room only," Virginia reports.

"Great. Hey, can you help me close out the concession cash register? I'm gonna have my hands full with the door take for a while, and I'd like to catch the end of the show."

"Sure," Virginia answers. "Ah, Sharon, I appreciate you calling me to come in tonight. I was feeling funny about storming out of the retreat last weekend. I just needed to cool off."

Sharon considers Virginia for a moment. "Virginia, you are a valuable member of this organization. We all respect your views."

"Not everyone," Virginia protests. "There is clearly a racist and sexist undercurrent running through this place."

"That's just not true." Sharon puts her hand on Virginia's. "I understand what you're saying about diversity. But *you* have to understand that the board of directors and management are doing everything they can to bring in a more diverse crowd."

Virginia shakes her head. "But none of it's any good unless we make people feel welcome when they *do* come here."

"I'm not arguing with you about that," Sharon says evenly, "but we need to work together to make sure that happens."

"I don't think everyone feels that way," Virginia counters.

"We all want this organization to survive, remember that."

"I don't want it to survive unless it reflects the interests of this community. Otherwise, what's the point?"

"I agree with you, Virginia. Look, help me with the concession drawer and after the show we'll go to Radway's for coffee. I want to continue this conversation, but right now we've got work to do."

"I know. I'm sorry," Virginia whines. "I'll get the drawer."

*   *   *

I strain to hear the conversation between Sharon and Virginia while I order and pay for my coffee. I know what they're talking about. Last week, at The Club's staff/board of directors retreat, Virginia became furious during a discussion about the need to draw a more diverse audience. Will, one of the night managers, mumbled a remark about giving away tickets to bluegrass shows to people of color, and Virginia attacked him.

"It's racist comments like this I'm talking about!" she shouted. "Some people in this organization *do not* want these people coming into The Club!"

"Will just meant that certain types of music draw certain types of audiences," Brian, The Club's managing director, explained. "It doesn't have anything to do with racism."

"I think I'd better leave."

"Virginia," Sharon said, "calm down!"

"I can't. Don't you see what's going on here?" she demanded, teary eyes searching the faces of her co-workers. They would not meet her gaze.

"Fine! Then I'll go!" She bolted from the couch and slammed the door behind her.

Those remaining sat stiffly, eyes on the floor. I'd been scrambling to record the exchange, and after Virginia left, I closed my notebook, uneasy. This was the first meeting I'd been invited to observe, and although I was intrigued, even excited by what happened, I felt I'd seen something I shouldn't have.

The meeting broke up quickly. As people said their good-byes and collected their potluck dishes, I busied myself clearing the table and returning chairs to their proper places. A few people sheepishly approached me, saying, "We're not usually that exciting," or "Did you get all that?"

The lights blink again. I shrug off the memory of the meeting and remind myself to write down the conversation between Sharon and Virginia when I get back to my seat.

By the time I skirt past the knees of those sitting in my row and sit down, Sharon is at the microphone, waiting for the crowd to quiet.

"Ladies and gentlemen," she says, "Lina Michaels!"

*   *   *

"I do this next song every night," Lina says. "It brings out the humbler person in me. . . . It says beauty is not about the outside—the body measurement—but about the size of the heart. I wrote it in the third person because I thought it could apply to many people. It's called 'Mama's Blues'."

✱

There are days when every bone in her body is achin'
When she feels like everyone hates her
And she cannot speak
And she sees herself as ugly
And unworthy of any love
That's mama's blues
Makes you wanna cry
That's mama's blues
Makes you wanna cry

And he looks at her like she's crazy
And he does not understand
He doesn't think she looks much different
Or much fatter than before
Yeah, she seems to look the same to him
And she's sad that he can't relate to her state of mind
That's mama's blues
. . . .
Now she's lookin' at her body in the mirror
And she's cryin' 'cause her waist
Is not as tiny as before the baby
And she feels like the world is at an end
And she thinks nobody is ever gonna
Want her body again

And he wonders what she wants from him
And he's sittin' drinkin' coffee at the breakfast stand
And he tells the waitress that it's lonely at home
And all the young girls take pity on him
Don't it make you wanna cry
Don't it make you wanna cry[9]

✱

"In her song," I write, "Lina's body—a woman's body—is the focus of the performance. Women's music, yes?" I play the words of the song over in my mind, turning them in a fractured dialectic of sight and sound, song and songwriter, artist and woman, object of desire and subject of contempt.

*   *   *

"My son Josh is graduating college this Saturday," Lina whispers into the microphone as she tunes her guitar.

"I told him something great always happens at home when I'm on the road. He says my calling his entire college career 'great' is a cruel joke. . . . Maybe it is."

The audience laughs. I peer through the crowd and catch sight of the bearded man in the front row. He's smiling and laughing. Maybe I'm being too hasty in my analysis?

"He's got a job with an environmental engineering company. I think that's wonderful, working for the environment." The crowd applauds.

"My son, he's pretty talented. He sings and acts. And now he's a college graduate. Sometimes I wonder if he *is* my son." The crowd laughs again.

"I wrote this next song on the road. It had to be written on the road. I'd like to dedicate it to Josh. 'Road To Mexico'."

*

I'm rolling down 10 West, all the way to Mexico,
And this highway burns a line into my brain,
With the headphones blasting music like a heart to pump my blood,
And the tears steaming down my face,
. . . .
Now I'm way down here in Texas and my heart just don't feel right,
Lord I'd beg, borrow, steal to get back home,
I'd give up all the money and I'd give away my name,
'Cause this traveling life is driving me insane.

I call myself a mother, but I feel just like a failure,
While I'm staring at the walls of this hotel.
I was feeling like a stranger when I called you on the phone,
What good am I if I can't be back home?

I'll be there for graduation, but that night I'm leaving town,
I can't seem to get my feet back on this ground,
There's always the pulling, the belief you should be going,
Another mile, another road, another town,
Another mile, another road, another town.[10]

✳

Colleen looks into Jerry's eyes and swallows hard. They listen to Lina's pleading voice through the thin walls of the dressing room. Colleen fakes a cough to keep her tears back. She goes to him and puts her head on his chest, wraps her arms around him.

"You couldn't swing it, huh?" Jerry asks, kissing her hair.

"I tried everything," Colleen says. "Even the chartered flight can't get her there 'til almost four."

"You'd think if you threw that much money at someone, they could get you where you want to go," Jerry says pulling away from her.

"You'd think, but it just ain't true. I don't know how to tell her. About the flight . . . about any of this." She looks at the floor, avoiding J.'s eyes.

"Don't you worry about it, hon," Jerry soothes. "I'll break it to her. Later. After the show."

Notes

1. Simone de Beauvoir, *All Said and Done* (London: Deutsch and Weidenfeld and Nicolson, 1974), 17.

2. Margot Mifflin, "The Fallacy of Feminism in Rock," *Rock She Wrote: Women Write About Rock, Pop, and Rap*, ed. Evelyn McDonnell and Ann Powers (New York: Delta, 1995), 77.

3. Jessamyn West, quoted in *The Quotable Woman*, vol. 2, ed. Elaine Partnow (Los Angeles: Pinnacle Books, 1977), 116.

4. Rory Block, "Ain't I A Woman," rec., *Ain't I A Woman*, Rounder, 1992.

5. bell hooks, *Ain't I a Woman: Black Women and Feminism* (Boston: South End Press, 1981).

6. Anne Marie Hunter, "Numbering the Hairs of Our Heads: Male Social Control and the All-Seeing Male God," *Journal of Feminist Studies in Religion* 8.2 (1992): 10–11, 14. The author writes, ". . . the intrusions and constant surveillance that are the common, everyday experience of many women in intimate relationships are deeply embedded in heterosexual gender norms in general. . . . Women are 'always public and thus always available for male intrusions that are seen as no intrusion at all but entirely legitimate behavior that only the strangely deviant among women could possibly object to'." She goes on to note that "I am convinced that male surveillance of women can no longer be dismissed as a benign subset of possessive and jealous behaviors. Surveillance is a technique of social control that is efficacious in its own right. In order to understand women's experiences, we must understand mechanisms of surveillance and social control."

7. Block, "Joliet Bound," rec., *When a Woman Gets the Blues*, Rounder, 1995.

8. Elizabeth Bell, "Toward a Pleasure-Centered Economy: Wondering a Feminist Aesthetics of Performance," *Text and Performance Quarterly* 15.2 (1995): 100, 114. In advocating a performer-centered (rather than text-centered) aesthetics of performance, the author writes that a performer-centered aesthetics is "grounded in the body, and specifically, in the material pleasures as a tensively negotiated economy of exchange among performer, audience, and text" (100). She goes on to note that "Locating the power of the performance in the performer necessitates teaching the politics of vision, spectatorship, and 'ways of seeing'."

9. Block, "Mama's Blues," rec., *Mama's Blues*, Rounder, 1991.

10. Block, "Road To Mexico," rec., *Ain't I A Woman*.

I like to sing for my friends. I don't want to sing in fucking stadiums. I like to be able to see who I'm singing to, look them right in the eye and talk to them.

Rosalie Sorrels, quoted in *The Quotable Woman*[1]

What is our investment in the 'safe place' of art, of these privileged objects we have come to love? . . . It matters to whom they belong and who is empowered to speak about them. It matters about whom *they* speak, and what they say.

Ruth Solie, *Musicology and Difference*[2]

Music is a human art, not a sexual one.

Thea Musgrave, quoted in *The Quotable Woman*[3]

"Who was the opening act?" a woman asks. "Some lesbian," a man responds.

Conversation overheard at The Club

3

Both/And

"MITCHELL!" I CALL from across the room.

"Hello!" Mitchell shouts over the conversations between us. Just then the lights blink twice, signaling the impending start of the show. "Let's talk during the break," he suggests.

I nod, then begin the journey to my seat through a dense sell-out crowd gathered for Cheryl Wheeler's performance. I'm both excited and relieved to see Mitchell. He's one of the first people I'd interviewed as part of my research, and I'd felt an immediate connection with him.

He'd talked ardently about his work as a musician and a music scholar. About his involvement with The Club. Our conversation quickly turned serious, personal.

"What happens to you when you perform?" I asked.

"For the kind of music I'm doing, a person's value system and his politics are immediately evident. . . . I've always felt like a political wimp because I'm terrified of confrontation. I'm not very good at expressing anger, except through music. That's why it's so important to me. When I perform, I express those feelings."

"How so?"

Mitchell sighed and said, "For me, the opportunity to be on stage, to have a hand in nurturing this community . . . means everything." He removed his glasses and looked me square in the eye. "It's a way for me to express my deepest values." Tears streamed down his cheeks.

He turned away from me and wiped his eyes as the wheels of the tape recorder turned, inscribing his emotion. I swallowed, pushing back the ache in my throat.

"I feel silly," Mitchell laughed. "Crying in front of someone I just met."

"I'm crying too," I said. We sat there for several minutes, considering our words, our emotions. Then I said, "Have you ever expressed these feelings to others at The Club?"

"The first night in the new location, I gave a speech of thanks about the value of the music, our community. It wasn't necessary to communicate that verbally, and it was difficult to do, just like now, because you can't talk about these things on a daily basis without having the meaning disappear."

"I don't know that it could disappear."

Ever since the interview, Mitchell and I had exchanged cards, letters, e-mail messages. He'd become a confidant and advisor, recommending books, responding to my fledgling ideas with encouragement and insight, helping me feel right about my work.

Seeing him here tonight, I want to ask about the confusing and contradictory messages I've been getting about women's music from club members and performers. "How would you characterize women's music?" I'd ask, and would be bewildered by the answers I'd get: "Lesbian music," some said flatly. Others were more descriptive, yet evasive: "Consciously political music" or "Music made by and for women." Some added, "But for men too."

The lights flash again. I pull out my pen and pad and steady myself for the onslaught of sight, sound, sensation.

*   *   *

Elaine paces in the hallway behind the stage. "Where's Donna?" she demands to no one. "Tonight's our big night, opening for Cheryl Wheeler . . . I've dreamed about this for months, and now Donna's nowhere to be found!" Her stomach grumbles. She stares at the crowd, then turns and busies herself tuning her guitar.

*   *   *

Sharon is preoccupied tonight. She'd passed a pensive-looking Elaine Baker on her way to the stage, but didn't stop to talk. Her thoughts are fixed on a letter from a long-time patron of The Club she'd read earlier in the day.

Marcus Taylor is a serious bluegrass fan. Occasionally, though, his wife, Ella, would bring him to The Club to hear world music and singer-songwriters. Last week they saw Lina Michaels' performance.

"Who *says* you can't teach an old dog new tricks," Sharon had told Virginia as they worked the concession counter that night.

"We'll see," Virginia said. "He never struck me as very open-minded."

Tonight Sharon marvels at Virginia's insight. Marcus' letter clearly voiced his disapproval—not about the music, but about the crowd.

"Never in my wildest dreams," Marcus wrote, "did I think The Club was putting on performances for the entertainment of deviants. Why must we cater to *queers* at the expense of other patrons? I find it unfair, indeed unacceptable, that The Club puts on these performances. The least management could do is warn patrons so they don't have to be party to such transgressions."

The letter made Sharon shudder. "How can he be a member of this community and be so intolerant?" she'd asked Virginia. "What does he want us to do?"

Sharon shakes her head as she ambles up the stairs to the stage to make her announcements and begin the show.

* * *

Elaine squints out at the crowd. They'd praised her first few songs with glowing applause, and their adoration makes her breath come fast.

"I'm really excited to be here, opening for Cheryl Wheeler. . . . I remember hearing Cheryl's song 'Addicted' on the radio when I was about eight years old. I learned to play that song on my guitar, and the rest is history." Her fingers move lightly over the strings, providing accompaniment for her story.

"I never really considered myself a political songwriter, though, until I wrote this next song. I guess the reason it's political is that my mother hates it."

She clears her throat and plays the opening bars softly. "I wrote this about two years ago when I met my partner, Donna. It's about respect."

Her guitar sends a delicate melody out over the crowd. Elaine adds her voice to harmonize. She sings, "You might hate my life, but I don't make the rules." Tears streak down her cheeks. As the last sounds of her song fade, the crowd praises her with applause.

"Thank you," she whispers. "Guess I better get outta' here. Cheryl will be out in a few minutes. Thank you very much." She crosses the stage and pounds down the stairs and into the back hallway. She bursts through the fire exit door and out into the night.

* * *

"Almost time," Cheryl muses as she lolls on the couch in the dressing room, a pillow over her eyes.

"Why did you drink so much last night?" she demands. No reply is offered, though, for she's alone in the room. "Well, better get your ass up off this couch and get out there," she prods, then hoists herself away from the cushions.

She peers in the mirror above the dressing table and fumbles with her hair. It's been a mess since she'd begun to gray. "You're forty-nine years old, Cheryl," she says to her reflection. "When you gonna give this up?"

She turns away from the mirror, pulling at the fatigue-green T-shirt she'd worn to The Club. "The day you get a job where you can wear this shitty green T-shirt to work." She laughs at her joke and slurps the last of a flat soda.

*   *   *

I jot down the lyrics of Elaine's song and write, "Young, clearly nervous. Songs deeply personal." The pen slips from the page, leaving a jagged exclamation point. I sit, thoughts racing. The performance certainly *feels* like women's music . . . but why?

I check The Club calendar announcement for the evening. No mention of "women's music." I'd read a good deal about this genre over the past few weeks, and Karen Petersen's words fill my head.[4]

I decide to make some quick notes: "Petersen says these musicians (feminists, lesbians, women) 'speak out about women's oppression by men, celebrate women's struggle to overcome this oppression, and the beauty of women loving women.' Seems to be the case here, but surely Elaine's music doesn't say this to everyone. Are people with different opinions, different positions, able to enjoy the show as much as these women? Is Elaine as explicit, even in her 'political' song, as Petersen suggests? Is her music an inherently 'political statement that expresses a *collective* musical unconsciousness'? Hmmm."

When I see Mitchell talking to Sharon near the concession counter, I abandon my thumbnail analysis. I buy a cup of coffee and join their conversation.

"So anyway," Mitchell says, "I'm finishing up this book editing job, and then I'm going to focus on material for the next album."

"Better see you on stage soon, Mitchell," Sharon says, pulling on his arm. "Been too long since you played here. You're probably getting rusty."

"Never," I interject.

"Our inquisitive graduate student," Sharon says, noticing me, and smiles. "How's the study coming?"

"Well, I've got lots of ideas," I say, stalling, "but I'm a bit confused about this whole women's music issue."

"I got your e-mail about that," Mitchell says. "I haven't written back because I have really mixed feelings about it."

"I have very *negative* feelings about it at the moment," Sharon interjects.

"Why?" I ask.

"We got a letter today. Mitchell, you know Marcus Taylor?"

"Yeah, sure. Bluegrass diehard."

"Right. Last week he and Ella were here for the Lina Michaels show. Then today we get a letter saying we're catering to *deviants* and that we should warn people when *queers* are going to be in the audience."

"Oh, Marcus," Mitchell says, shaking his head.

"Sounds a bit extreme," I offer.

"It's ridiculous!" Sharon huffs. "And the disturbing thing is, he's not alone."

"Certainly not," says Mitchell.

"What do these people want us to do?" Sharon complains. "Put a little symbol or something in the calendar? Give me a break! We already use the category of women's music to let people know there may be a largely lesbian audience."

I'm confused. "How does that let people know?"

"Well," Sharon begins, "the term 'women's music' used to be synonymous with Olivia Records and Redwood Records, women-run labels that featured lesbian musicians and lesbian themes." She pauses, then adds, "Although women's music has certainly broadened quite a bit."

"The problem I have is that the term signals music that focuses on political and social issues," Mitchell offers, pulling at his beard. "And I'm sorry to say it, but in my experience, music that has to pass a political test is very seldom musically or artistically satisfying."

"So," I ask, "it's politics first, music second?"

"Sometimes the music's a distant second," Mitchell says.

Sharon wrinkles her nose. "I love a lot of women's music."

"I'm generalizing," Mitchell says. "I've heard some really lovely, powerful music from performers whose careers began in the women's music circuit."

Sharon nods. "And as a feminist, I think it's an important component of the music we offer at The Club."

"Sharon, you know I am very much a feminist when it comes to recognizing that women are an oppressed majority," Mitchell explains. "I don't want to sound preachy here, but I believe that women's contributions to musical creativity have been unfairly limited in many cultures and parts of the world."

"We all do," Sharon says. "But what do we do about the homophobics in *our* community?"

"I don't have the answer," he says, then adds, "but in the Bay Area, more than anywhere else in the industrialized world, women are accepted as instrumentalists, composers, vocalists. . . ."

"And yet we've got this mentality of exclusion, difference," Sharon counters.

Mitchell sighs. "But we don't want to single out women or men based on gender, sexuality, or any other way. That's what we don't want to have happen."

"Isn't there some sort of middle ground?" I ask.

He shrugs.

"Everyone has an opinion," Sharon says. "Some people think women's music is nothing more than a marketing category; some think it's music about women's issues that women really *identify* with, more so than men."

"And some people think it's political, and therefore discriminatory and dangerous," Mitchell adds.

"Can you reconcile these competing interests?" I ask.

"I don't think we can, sweetie," Sharon soothes. "It's up to the performer and the audience to decide."

"And what about people like Mr. Taylor?" I press.

"Ah, Marcus," Sharon sighs, shakes her head.

Mitchell pats my arm. "You let us know when you've got it figured out," he chuckles. "I've got to get some coffee before Cheryl comes on. Let's keep talking about this." He moves toward the concession counter.

"We'll have to," I call after him, then turn to face Sharon.

"I sure haven't got any answers for you," she says.

"Maybe I'm not asking the right questions."

"If you're not, you will. I'd better get up there and introduce Cheryl. Good talking to you. And good luck."

"Thanks, Sharon."

I stop to look at the posters announcing upcoming acts. As I scan the stark black-and-white photos, strains of a conversation pull my attention from wistful faces.

"Who was the opening act?" a woman asks.

"Some lesbian," a man responds.

I whirl around, but the words vanish in the crowd. I find my seat and make a few quick notes.

"Amazing," I write. "Will I ever figure this out?"

*　　*　　*

Donna rushes through the crowd, catching brief glimpses of Elaine's fringed jacket as it swings down the stage steps. The jacket disappears in the darkness of the hallway and she follows it, the "exit only" sign illuminating her path. She thrusts both hands toward the lever holding the door in place and breathes deep when the night air hits her.

"Elaine?" Donna calls into the darkness. "You out here?" Silence.

"What do *you* care?" Elaine finally says.

Donna still can't see her. "Where are you?"

"Here," she seethes, skirting around the corner of the building.

They stand in silence, clouds of exhaled air hovering between them.

"So you decided to show," Elaine says.

Donna sighs. "I saw your set. I came in just as the lights went down, so I sat with Julie at the sound board. Didn't think you wanted me tromping up to the front row while you were playing."

"Jesus, Donna. I thought you could be on time just once!"

Donna's breath catches in her throat. "I was *here*."

"I didn't know that. You knew how important tonight was. I wanted us to do this together!"

"That's *bullshit* and you know it. I was here for you. I was out there cheering for you. It was your decision to do this."

"And I did it alone! I was up there in front of all those people, and I was *alone*."

"It's your music. It's your story. You had to do it alone. This was about getting on stage and coming to terms with *your* choices and *your* life."

"It's our life . . . or at least I thought it was."

"It *is* our life," Donna says, reaching for her. Their words hang in the air for several moments, then scatter with the sound of muffled applause from inside The Club.

"Better get back in there," Elaine says.

*   *   *

"I have a big problem with the Religious Right," Cheryl says, a giggle escaping through her smile. "I'm very intolerant of their intolerance. And every time I see someone from the NRA on TV, I just want to shoot them!"

"The audience laughs," I write. "In between songs, they turn up the lights. I've never noticed this at The Club before. Cheryl must want to see who she's talking to."

"I wrote this next song, 'Act of Nature,' right after a terrible storm came through our town," she explains. "They named this storm Hurricane *Bob*. What kind of a name is that? This storm, Bob, *killed* people. They should have named it Newt." More chuckles from the crowd.

She plays the first few bars of the song, then stops and looks out over the audience. "The day Bob came through our town was the same day my domestic scene came apart . . . It was hard not to notice the similarities." She closes her eyes and begins to play.

*

> *The wind came 'round and blew this place apart*
> *It's you and me now sitting in the dark*
> *The lights are out and everybody's home*
> *It's you and me and we are both alone*

The lines are down there's just no getting through
You stare at me and I stare back at you

And in the dark I know that I can't see
'Cause here you are still don't see me

Act of nature, act of God
Raging though our sedentary lives
We are on the brink
We are floundering
Spinning in this dark and rising tide
The storm has blown this great big beauty down
The branches all confusion on the ground
I've watched it grow and thought I knew it well
And I never dreamed I'd see the day it fell
. . . .
The wind came 'round and blew this place apart. . . .[5]

*

Cheryl ends the song with a flourish of fingertips across the strings.

Strong, yet somber applause. "God, you guys are so quiet and attentive," she teases, breaking the serious mood. "A few years back, I lost my mind for a while. The doctors said it was a midlife crisis. I don't know how they knew it was a midlife crisis since I haven't died yet."

Laughter plays across the audience. "But when we got James, our new puppy, he picked me right away. I called my doctor and said, 'I'm well. The puppy likes me best.'"

*   *   *

My head is pounding. "That ethnographer's headache Nick's always talking about," I joke aloud, deciding to retreat to the women's restroom and collect my thoughts.

I make my way past the stares of annoyed onlookers. Ensconced in the pink stall, I prop my notebook on my knees.

"This is so odd," I write. "Obviously Elaine and Cheryl could be 'some lesbians' as the man said, but they're not radical, militant. They're certainly not cramming it down our throats. How can *I* talk about women's music? It's different for every single person here. What could I possibly say about these performances that would make sense to members of this organization? The audiences? The artists? My thesis committee?"

"Damn," I say. "What am I doing? What do *I* know?"

I reconsider. I do know that women's music artists and audiences have always struggled to balance feminist and lesbian concerns—to create "shared values" and a "shared identity" while appealing to a diverse community.[6] This dialectic of identity and difference is exacerbated in "mainstream" environments, places like The Club in which identity and values and community—audiences, employees, and musicians—are even more diverse. I decide to spend a few minutes writing through this idea so that I don't lose it.

"Political, social, and musical goals exist in mutable relationship," I write. "In some women's music performances, politics may be featured, while social and musical goals are inexplicit, opaque. In other performances, music may be the primary goal, with social and political concerns as a by-product or backdrop. Whatever the relationship, the music is concerned with women's experience, whether it celebrates, complicates, or critiques that experience. What's significant about the relationship among political, social, and musical goals and women's experience is the ways they are enacted through performance.

"Even more interesting are multiple configurations of political, social, and musical goals that might be achieved in any given performance. Maybe these performances could be described as postmodern? Connor[7] describes postmodern architecture as allowing multiple ways of reading into its very form—the architecture almost 'reads itself in advance.' Certainly music, like art and architecture, makes multivalent meanings and readings possible. Let's see. . . .

"Marcus, Sharon, Mitchell, Elaine, and Cheryl all participate in the same performance, yet come away with very different impressions. Marcus may be angry that 'his' place is catering to 'queers.' Sharon and Mitchell may support the performers because of the statement they make about women in music, but they may be uncomfortable at the same time. As a manager, Sharon tries to negotiate within the spaces of the socio-political discourse of performers and patrons. And as a musician, Mitchell questions the musical agenda of some performers. Elaine may see these performances as an opportunity to create and speak out within the lesbian community, for personal, socio-political, and musical reasons. Cheryl may want nothing more than to share her music, and her life, with her friends. These performances may at once 'criticize and dissent as well as accept'. . . .[8]

"What about me?" I challenge. "I can 'see' and experience all of these things . . . and yet how do I put these thoughts, these feelings, into words? How do I write about what I observe, what I talk about with Mitchell and Sharon, what I hear in the voices of Elaine and Cheryl? Do I categorize? Do I interpret? Do I criticize? Can I *capture* the experience? Do I even want to?"

I hear Cheryl say, "Thank you. Good night," through the walls of my appropriated office. I hurry from the women's restroom to catch the encore.

*   *   *

"Did I wait long enough?" Cheryl jokes, emerging from the dressing room almost immediately after she'd disappeared into it.

A man waits at the edge of the stage with a heaving bouquet of orchids. Cheryl bends to receive the gift, extending her arms for an unsteady embrace. She spreads the orchids on the piano and moves to the microphone.

"Thank you so much," she says. "No matter how long I do this, I'm always surprised at how much fun it is. Thank you."

Applause interrupts her, and she waits. "I'd like to play a song for you that I wrote for my dad's seventy-fifth birthday. It's called 'Get it Yourself, Fatso'." Laughter again erupts in the room.

"Actually, it's called '75 Septembers.' Come to think of it, I've been playing here for about that long."

*

In the year of the yellow cab
Shadow of the great world war
The third kid grandmom had
Came into this world
On a rolling farm in Maryland
When Wilson was the president
As summer blew her goodbye through the trees

A child of changing times
Growing up between the wars
Fords rolled off the lines
And bars all closed their doors
And I imagine you back then
With snap brim hat and farmer's tan
Where horses drew their wagons through the fields

Now the fields are all four lanes
And the moon's not just a name
Are you more amazed at how things change
Or how they stay the same
And do you sit here on this porch and wonder
How the time flies by
Or does it seem to barely creep along
With 75 Septembers come and gone[9]

. . . .

*

"Thank you," Cheryl smiles in the glow of applause. "As always, it was a pleasure. See you next year."

Once in the dressing room, Cheryl plops down on the couch and rests her head on the cushions, a silly smile painting her lips.

"Ah, Dad. You shoulda' been here," she says to no one. "You shoulda' been here."

*　　*　　*

"Good night. . . . See you soon. . . . Drive carefully—it's foggy out there," Sharon says to friends and strangers who pass on their way into the night. She smiles as Mitchell approaches. "Good to see you, Mitchell."

"Good to see you, Sharon. Don't let Marcus get you down."

"Oh, I won't. We'll get through to him yet. Keep in touch." Mitchell pats her arm, then strides away. I follow quickly behind.

"Sharon, thanks again. I really enjoyed the show."

"My pleasure, sweetie. Let me know next time you're in town. I'd like to hear more about your project."

"Sure. This should help." I flash the CD I'd just purchased. "The calendar was right."

Sharon laughs. "I did the calendar write-up. So, let's see . . . 'By the time the night's over you'll want Cheryl to move to your town, buy the house next door, and become your new best friend?' "

"Yeah . . . I do! I'll call you soon, Sharon."

*　　*　　*

I stare at the blank computer screen, unsure where to begin. The sights and sounds of last night's performances play over and over in my head. I know I need to write about the experience while it's still fresh . . . but I feel too close to it, want some distance. How do I separate myself from this process? How do I create a vantage point from which to understand and explain? Pushing away these uncomfortable questions, I place my fingers on the keys.

Fieldnotes . . . .

12.9.95
The Club, 8–11:30 p.m.

Last night I went to Elaine Baker's and Cheryl Wheeler's show. It was a good show and a great night. I talked to Mitchell and

Sharon about women's music, got some good notes from the show, did a little writing in the women's restroom—a room of one's own. A place where no one gets suspicious about me scribbling in my notebook.

When I was theorizing in my pink office, I realized something. All this time, I'd been looking for differentiation, hierarchy, and domination in women's music performances—but that's all I was looking for. Sure, these elements *are* present in how artists, members, and patrons single out these performances by labeling them, coding and appropriating the music with socio-political significance, and thus, attempting to control the meanings created. Discourses which work to control the meanings of women's music performances are differentiating and dominating because they are naturalized in the performance. Kristin Langellier, Kathryn Carter, and Darlene Hantzis describe the power discourses of control exert in performance: "performance is grounded not only on a male-as-norm but also heterosexual-as-norm, thereby maintaining 'compulsory heterosexuality' and muting homosexual existence" (94).

How are discourses of male-as-norm and heterosexual-as-norm evidenced in women's music performances at The Club? In the precedence and preference given to male and heterosexual interests by participants (performers, members, and audiences). For example, performers use gender-neutral or inclusive language (introducing her song "Ain't I A Woman," Lina Michaels says, "the second, third, and fourth verses are about *women*, but they are also about many, many *people*"). Women's music performances are "coded" in The Club's calendar, and thus, differentiated from the norm. Letters are written by patrons to protest variation in the sexual orientation of audiences. This discursive precedence and preference for maleness and heterosexuality cast women's music performances as *different*.

But how is difference played out in performance? Kenneth Burke's notion of hierarchy offers the beginnings of an explanation. He asserts that "the differences among members of a hierarchy arise not only from the separateness of their physical bodies but also from their different modes of life" (Foss, Foss, and Trapp 192). Differences in physical bodies, modes of life, and thus, *discourses* and *performances*, serve to differentiate and subordinate women's music—to manipulate the "musical meaning" of these performances (Robertson 225).

As the nameless, faceless patron illustrates, a heartfelt and skillful performance can be reappropriated by using simple, yet socially loaded discourse for the artist ("some lesbian") or the music ("lesbian music"). Cynthia Lont notes that while "women's music" has emerged as the most inclusive and least socially charged phrase among industry representatives, artists, and audiences (as opposed to expressions such as "lesbian music," "women-identified music," and "womansong"), it is still a term that serves as a "password" for lesbian and feminist communities ("Between Rock and a Hard Place" 94). These meanings are then carried over to, and written on, the performances—the bodies—of women musicians.

But there's more to it than that. . . . While differentiation and domination are certainly possibilities in women's music performances at The Club, these shows may also work to resist and change male-as-norm and heterosexual-as-norm assumptions. Karen Petersen writes that women's music is, "by virtue of its very existence, a political statement" (205). Originating in the 1970s with the work of Holly Near, Meg Christian, Cris Williamson, and Margie Adam, and the creation of the women-run music labels like Olivia and Redwood Records, women's music reacted to and resisted the "exclusive, oppressive, and alienating" mainstream musical community. These artists and labels created instead a vibrant and supportive female musical community (206), a community that "had faith in a universal female sensibility" (Sutton 30). Such "women's communities" were built on a radical and, later, cultural feminist agenda concerned with developing *alternative* feminist institutions and women's culture (Staggenborg, Eder, and Sudderth 32–33). Creating alternative music, musical institutions, and musically driven cultural events became and continues to be a central activity of cultural feminists.

Thus, in addition to exploring lesbian sexuality, women's music also explores women's oppression and women's struggle to resist this oppression (Petersen 206). Mavis Bayton asserts that feminism has "acted as a major route of access" for women's music-making (177). However, early women's music and the advent of annual women's music events such as the Michigan Women's Music Festival, New England Women's Musical Retreat, and the National Women's Music Festival in the 1980s and 1990s have come under fire from some feminists (most notably Marxist and materialist feminists) as escapist and incapable of effecting material change in women's lives. The cultural feminism celebrated at women's music performances and festivals is viewed as a "means of escape from mainstream society" that disregards the material barriers to women's liberation (Staggenborg, Eder, and Sudderth 33).

However, as Staggenborg, Eder, and Sudderth point out, political action cannot be separated from the creation of community; that "personal and political change are interwoven" (43). Within this community, the essence of women's music is realized: the creation of "musical and visual narratives that celebrate multiple rather than unitary identities, that are concerned with ecstatic continuation rather than purging and containment" (McClary quoted in Sutton 34). In sharing these narratives, feminist desires, values, and lifestyles are celebrated and expanded. In *performance*, change is made possible.

In and through the women's music presented there, The Club may provide this access and make a space for a vibrant, supportive women's community. Indeed, Mitchell and Sharon note that The Club is part of a unique Bay Area music scene in which women are respected, important, and powerful participants in the artistic community. Further, possibilities for resistance and change may be realized within the brick and mortar of The Club. Resistance and change are made possible in women's music *performances* because they violate male-as-norm and heterosexual-as-norm expectations. Elizabeth Bell, drawing on Judith Butler's ideas, notes that women, especially those who "do not perform their genders correctly," can create performances that challenge socially constructed systems of meaning by making the implicit, invisible "politics of sexuality exposed and felt."[10] Women's music performances at The Club may encompass many such "challenges," and, further, these challenges may be advanced by performers and audiences alike—Elaine may sing lyrics that point to her lesbian identity, Virginia may speak out about sexism and racism, and female audience members may sing along and, later, work together to break down the categories and realities of oppression. But how?

By singing and talking about issues that are important to women, and performing roles that are not traditional for women, performers (and I mean all involved in the event) "prioritize" women's issues and roles, and thus challenge the male, "taken for granted" dominance in performance (Bayton 181). The voices and bodies of women's music artists highlight the importance of the feminine *in* performance and challenge the male-as-norm and heterosexual-as-norm assumptions *of* performance. When we hear and watch female performers, the cultural opposition of an active male subject (viewer) and passive female object (performer) are at once evoked and rewritten and revoiced. As Carolyn Abbate notes, "visually, the [woman] singing is the passive object of our gaze. But aurally, she is resonant; her musical speech drowns out everything in range" (254). A woman's body also becomes an active presence in live performance—the artist stands before her audience having claimed the male composing voice for her own (Abbate 254).

But perhaps nothing *politically or socially significant*—domination nor resistance—is accomplished in these performances. Might women's music performances focus solely on the musical significance of the event—skillful playing, masterful songwriting, strong arrangement? Rosalie Sorrels, a women's music artist and frequent

Club performer, writes of her early experiences at The Club in the monthly calendar: "It was a warm, friendly place that maintained a standard of musical excellence while providing me and many others with a supportive environment in which we could develop our art."

Mitchell reminds me that for many, the music is what's important. So does the bearded man who complained about not being able to see Lina Michaels' hands. While at one level his complaint can be construed as a demand for surveillance, at another it may be the simple request of a musician attempting to develop his art, the expectation that the performer—man or woman—display artistic skill (Bauman 11).

However, for women performers, socio-political motivations may provide a means—perhaps the only means—to achieve musical goals. Bayton asserts that feminism gives women musicians "confidence and support," indeed, provides *motivation* to pursue their musical aspirations and make the transition from "fan to performer" (178). This may be the case for Elaine, who heard Cheryl Wheeler's music on the radio as a child and was inspired to pursue her own musical interests. What is clear is that for some participants, music serves as the unifying element—joining together those with diverse interests, viewpoints, and motivations—and allowing all to take part in, and take something away from, the performance. Here, the musician is the instrument of the audience's experience, "dis/covering" and "un/covering" herself so that she "re/veals" something of "woman" (adapted from Vanden Heuvel 30). Further, this uncovering and revelation of "woman" is not the woman of patriarchy or, exclusively, heterosexuality, but instead the woman of community, difference, artistry, and resistance.

Is there a way to accommodate such diverse readings within women's music performances? The notion of cultural capital helps make sense of the multiple possibilities of performance. While the creation of cultural capital is an "accumulation of meanings and pleasures that serves the interests of the . . . disempowered . . .

meanings that validate the social experience of the subordinate" (19), Fiske writes that creation of such capital requires:

> ...a critical understanding of the text and the conventions by which it is constructed . . . the bringing of both textual and social experience to bear upon the [music] at the moment of reading...a constant and subtle negotiation and renegotiation of the relationship between the textual and the social (19).

As texts, women's music may be described as accommodating and creating various overlapping, yet separate competenc*ies* and cultural capit*als*. In performance, these texts help create a complex network of competing interests and viewpoints that intersect and collide, are accommodated and resisted, are given voice and muted (Conquergood, "Poetics, Play, Process, and Power" 84).

But how are such varied and changing readings accomplished? Again, I believe the answer lies in the performance—in the fact that the performers are women, and further, that they are women whose sexual orientation is at best unknown and at worst, suspect. This creates a performative "strangeness" necessary to open up the possibility of alternative interests and viewpoints, competencies and capitals. Burke's idea of "mystery" helps me understand this strangeness. In *A Rhetoric of Motives* he writes:

> ...mystery arises at that point where different *kinds* of beings are in communication. In mystery there must be *strangeness*; but the estranged must also be thought of as in some way capable of communion (115).

Music *teaches* of the communion in strangeness, in difference. Friedrich Nietzsche captures the pedagogy of musical strangeness in "One Must Learn to Love":

> This is what happens to us in music: First one has to learn to hear a figure and melody at all, to detect and distinguish it, to isolate it and delimit it as a separate life. Then it requires some exertion and good will to tolerate it in spite of its strangeness, to be patient with its appearance and expression, and kind-hearted about its oddity. Finally there comes a moment when

we are used to it, when we wait for it, when we sense that we should miss it if it were missing. . . . That is how we have learned to love. . . (262).

Perhaps the strangeness in music opens up spaces for multiple and fluid readings of women's performances at The Club. Thus, while some may refuse to learn, understanding these performances as deviant and reaffirming the notion of male-as-norm and heterosexual-as-norm, others may come to accept—to *love*—them as opportunities for resistance and change.

But how do I learn to love, then write, the mystery and complexity of these performances? Might their strangeness be conveyed by conceiving of—and writing about—them as postmodern? Let's see. . . . Jane Flax notes that tales of postmodernism are advanced in opposition to the story of Enlightenment, which privileges rational thought, Truth as knowledge of the real and unchanging nature of the world, a trinity of reason, autonomy, and freedom upheld by a discourse of legitimate power and authority (30). Within this "culture of truth," scientific inquiry posits a detached observer, one able to comprehend and explain Truth through the transparent medium of language (31). Even where social relations are concerned, language is simply a naming convention, not a social construction (31).

What, then, are tales of postmodernism? While these tales are many, they are united in an attention to the nature of knowledge and its role in power relations, how dominance and control are practiced and can be overcome, how individuals and societies conceptualize and experience subjectivity and the self, and how the notion of difference is conceived, practiced, preserved, and rescued (Flax 188). Laurel Richardson synthesizes these tales by describing a postmodern *sensibility* that doubts that "any discourse has a privileged place, any method or theory a universal and general claim to authoritative knowledge" ("Postmodern Social Theory" 173). Within this sensibility, social inquiry focuses on the "particular, ethnocentric interests and social role" of the discourses of everyday life (Seidman 187). Tales of postmodernism are contradictory, complex, inconclusive, rich, frustrating, deep experiences of culture.

How does a postmodern sensibility influence the way I approach the study of culture? How does it attend to the mystery and complexity of women's music performances? First, a postmodern sensibility implies that women's music performances at The Club do not "suggest one reading or the other, but embrace even contradictory interpretations" (Blair, Jeppeson, and Pucci 371). The voices, thoughts, feelings, and textures of Elaine's and Cheryl's performances blur and coalesce into an intricate and conflicting collage of culture that begins in these fieldnotes, but ultimately extends beyond them. It means I must aim to "capture the mood" and "restructure the experience" of The Club and women's music performances (Tyler 135), all the while understanding that these performances are multiple; they are experiences co-constructed in the interaction of the performer and audience.

A postmodern sensibility recommends approaching these performances not within the authoritarian, universalizing, and fixed "either–or" Enlightenment framework, but instead, within the rebellious, open-ended, processual, postmodern sensibility of *both/and* (Blair, Jeppeson, and Pucci 372). My readings of these performances must "criticize and dissent, as well as accept" (Connor 29); they must create and obscure experience, meaning, knowledge . . . all within the confines of language. And yet it seems worth trying, worth the effort to *evoke*, to *perform* rather than *re-present* these readings, these performances. Worth trying to create a text that waits for, and hears, both/and.

An evocative, both/and text means, as Art Bochner and Carolyn Ellis note, standing *within* what I study—within the culture and the music—and writing about the experience of women's performances from that vantage point (19). And writing means using language that is not transparent, but charged with socially constructed meaning. Here, "language sits in for life . . . the world as we 'know' it cannot be separated from the language we use to explain, understand, or describe it" (19, 20). How might I use language to stand within—to perform—an evocative text? A text that speaks through, of, and to the mystery and music of women? Of The Club? . . . Make it multiple, duplicitous, changing. Learn to love the strangeness. As Nietzsche teaches about music, *this is what happens to us in ethnography.* . . .

And still I want to ask whether various readings and evocations—mine along with Mitchell's and Sharon's and Elaine's and Cheryl's—exist in any sense of harmony with one another. There is certainly some *semblance* of harmony in women's music performances, although, as in music, harmony does not guarantee a single tonal pattern but, instead, diverse and intersecting sounds. Perhaps, as participants in these performances, we are somehow able to reconcile disparate views by focusing on the musical *communion* these performances offer (Burke 115)? Perhaps music teaches within the mystery of performance. And perhaps the mystery of music lies in those moments when man and woman, homosexual and heterosexual, performer and audience, understand each other in some inexpressible fashion (Burke 115).

· ·

I print the fieldnotes and lean back in my chair to review them.

"Such a tidy ending," I say, disappointed. Nietzsche, Burke, Bell, Tyler, and the others have helped me frame my talk about women's music performances at The Club. The literature on postmodernism and ethnography is full of possibility, but these words seem so far away from Mitchell's and Sharon's concerns, Elaine's and Cheryl's voices. So far away from me. So far away from the passion of performance.

I forget the notes on the desk and hurry into the next room to reset the CD player. I stretch out on the couch and close my eyes. Cheryl's voice fills the room, tells of a car trip along eastern highways. I marvel at the clarity of thought and emotion woven by her voice, her words, her fingers on the strings. Turning leaves float by as if I were there with her, watching from the back seat. *This* is an evocative text. . . . But it is Cheryl's experience. How can I know it as she does? I've never even been to Pennsylvania.

And yet this song belongs to me. I sing it to myself on nights when I stay too late at my desk, then go to bed with thoughts racing and no hope of sleep. This song, this music, is poetry. It evokes characters, thoughts, and voices. I remember reading somewhere that a poem is not simply a text, but an *event* that happens between a reader and a text.[11] A coming together. Music is also an event, whether it happens in my living room or on stage at The Club. It is a poetic performance.

I sit up. Maybe this ethnography is a *performance* that happens between not just one reader and one text, but between all of us—me, and members of The Club, and performers, and audiences, and *you*, the reader—in music, and interviews, conversations, and poetry. And maybe I can't write just one text, no matter how evocative. Maybe . . . I need to write multiple texts, multiple performances. . . .

"Write the *story*," Nick's voice says, interrupting my thoughts.

I push myself from the couch and wander into the kitchen. "All I know," I explain to left-over spaghetti, "is I can't get enough of these songs . . . can't stop thinking about women's music . . . can't quite write those performances . . . can't do anything but try."

Notes

1. Rosalie Sorrels, quoted in *The Quotable Woman: An Encyclopedia of Useful Quotations*, ed. Elaine Partnow, vol. 2 (Los Angeles: Pinnacle, 1977), 375.
2. Ruth A. Solie, ed., "Introduction: On 'Difference'," *Musicology and Difference: Gender and Sexuality in Music Scholarship* (Berkeley: University of California Press, 1993), 20.
3. Thea Musgrave, quoted in *The Quotable Woman: An Encyclopedia of Useful Quotations*, ed. Elaine Partnow, vol. 2 (Los Angeles: Pinnacle, 1977), 320.
4. Karen Petersen, "An Investigation into Women-Identified Music in the United States," *Music and Women in Cross-Cultural Perspective*, ed. Ellen Koskoff (New York: Greenwood, 1987), 205–206.
5. Cheryl Wheeler, "Act of Nature," rec., *Driving Home*, Philo, 1993.
6. Donna Eder, Suzanne Staggenborg, and Lori Sudderth, "The National Women's Music Festival: Collective Identity and Diversity in a Lesbian-Feminist Community," *Journal of Contemporary Ethnography*, 23.4 (1995): 485–86. The authors note two "distinct purposes" in the community-building work that takes place at the festival. One purpose is to "create spaces where lesbians can interact safely and where a positive collective identity for lesbians is affirmed." The second purpose is more far-reaching: to create "feminist communities" that mirror the "social organization"—one of caring, solidarity, respect for difference, and active participation—that "feminists would like to see exist throughout the society."
7. Stephen Connor, *Postmodern Culture: An Introduction to Theories of the Contemporary* (Oxford: Basil Blackwell, 1989), 72.
8. Connor, 29.
9. Wheeler, "75 Septembers," rec., *Driving Home*, Philo, 1993.
10. Elizabeth Bell, "Toward a Pleasure-Centered Economy: Wondering a Feminist Aesthetics of Performance," *Text and Performance Quarterly* 15.2 (1995): 116. The author discusses this possibility for challenge and resistance in terms of the visual and the "boundedness of the visual in performance." She makes this argument by drawing on the work of Laura Mulvey ("Visual Pleasure and Narrative Cinema," *Art After Modernism: Rethinking Representation*, ed. Brian Wallis. New York: New Museum of Contemporary Art, 1984; 361–74) and bell hooks (*Black Looks: Race and Representation*, Boston, South End Press, 1992). However, I believe this argument can be extended to a conception of performance as discourse, which, of course, considers the visual and the politics of seeing.

11. Louise Rosenblatt, "The Transactional Theory: Against Dualisms," *College English* 55.4 (1993): 380, 382. The author writes that "we might refer to reader, text, and poem, but each was an aspect of a relationship occurring at a particular time under particular circumstances. . . . Meaning emerges from the reverberations of all these elements upon one another."

I am a being of desire, therefore a being of words . . . who looks for her body and looks for the body of the other: for me, this is the whole history of writing.

Nicole Broussard, quoted in "Setting Words Free"[1]

•
•
•
•

I'll fight them as a woman, not a lady/Fight them as an engineer.

"I'm Gonna Be an Engineer,"[2] song performed at The Club

•
•
•
•

It seems to me that the music itself—especially as it intersects with the body and destabilizes accepted norms of subjectivity, gender, and sexuality—is precisely where the politics of music often reside.

Susan McClary, "Same As It Ever Was: Youth Culture and Music"[3]

•
•
•
•

Music is . . . a shared skin.

Barbara Engh, *Loving It*[4]

4

Engineering the Feminine

"WHEN I WAS living in England, we began the women's peace camp at Greenham Commons," Patty explains to the audience, her clipped British accent confirming the account.

"Greenham was part of the common lands preserved by the aristocracy for subsistence of the poorer classes. During World War II, the longest airstrip in Britain was constructed on this land, and in the 1980s, nuclear missiles were placed there."

"Patty is Paul Sanders' sister," I whisper to my husband, Don. He nods. This, I think, will clue him in to the social and political content of the show.

"Our protest started out by knocking down the picket fence around the installation and grew to throwing mattresses and blankets over barbed wire that topped tall concrete walls, then climbing over. Or else cutting the chain-link fences with bolt cutters. If you've never handled a pair of bolt cutters, you ought to. They're very satisfying."

"The audience laughs," I write, laughing too. Patty is fiftyish, wears a ribbed body suit and flowing gauze skirt that accentuate her muscular frame. Silver hair radiates around her face. I feel a surge of electricity play on my skin. I'm listening to Patty Sanders, a member of one of folk music's first families and author of an anthem for the women's movement.

"Will she play 'Engineer'?" I murmur.

"Hmm?" Don says, not hearing me.

"On the day I wrote this next song," Patty continues, "our goal was to circle the commons with women holding hands. And what happened, you couldn't believe. *Thirty thousand* women wrapped themselves twice around Greenham Commons. And they held hands and sang songs of protest."

* * *

"Did you see this?" asks Brian, managing director of The Club, holding up a page of notebook paper jammed with an erratic, cursive scrawl.

Sharon squints, immediately recognizing Virginia's long loops and awkward slant. "Let me take off my coat first," she stalls.

"It's a letter of apology from Virginia," Brian says. "It was on my desk when I got in this morning. Apparently she sent it to all the board members and taped a copy to the front counter." Brian sighs. He pulls at his glasses and folds them with a crush of his hand.

"An apology for what?" Sharon asks, eyes focused on the letter. Brian thrusts it toward her.

"For what happened at the retreat, her attacking Will, saying he's racist, storming off." His words tumble out, one on top of the other.

"Does she *say* that she called Will a racist?"

"No," Brian shakes his head. "She says her behavior was inappropriate, then rambles on about diversity and our closed community."

"She's really concerned about this, Brian."

"We're all concerned about it. But what Virginia doesn't see is that cultivating an entirely new audience means putting on losing shows." Brian slumps into his chair, turns away from her. "This organization can't survive long enough to generate new audiences. We're living hand to mouth as it is."

"Maybe you should talk to her?" Sharon urges. "I've tried, but maybe coming from you. . . ."

Brian wheels around to face her. "I'm the enemy here. I'm the one vetoing these bookings because we can't break even. Ricky books shows every week that won't make a cent. Sometimes I think I'm the only one who remembers we're running a business here, that as much as we'd like to, we can't separate artistic and business decisions."

"I think that's what Virginia's saying," Sharon interjects. "She works the losing shows . . . she believes diversification is simply a matter of making better booking decisions."

"You know that's not going to change." Brian picks up a stack of mail and fumbles through it. "I manage the *business*. Ricky manages the *bookings*."

"I know it's more complicated than what Virginia sees," Sharon says.

"We start losing sight of the music," Brian says forcefully. "Hell, I'm a performer. I understand the importance of how things are presented here. And I'm frustrated because Ricky books The Club. Period."

Sharon sits down across from Brian. Silence swells between them. "So what are you going to do about Virginia's letter?" she says.

"Nothing. Virginia's had her say."

"But the staff should know what you're facing here . . . the reasons behind the booking decisions. Maybe they could help?"

"No sense dragging everyone into it."

"They've got a legitimate interest in this," Sharon persists. "Making our entire community feel welcome here, not just white, middle-aged people, but *everyone*, is important to all of us."

"But where does it end? It's not just whether the performers are diverse, or our audience is diverse. Today I had to complete a survey for the state Arts Council. They wanted to know how many Hispanics, Asians, and handicapped people we employ. How many gays and lesbians."

"*What?*"

"It was part of a funding application. We don't ask employees or performers about their sexual orientation. What does that have to do with anything? I don't want to take money from an organization that asks those kinds of questions."

"What are they thinking?" Sharon asks, shaking her head.

"I have no idea."

*   *   *

"I recognize a lot of singers in the audience tonight," Patty says, tuning her banjo as she stands at the mike in The Club. "Singers who take the stage for causes—for rain forests and owls, folks in wheelchairs, the right to vote. The right to choose your lot in life." She hugs the banjo close.

"I wrote this next song to answer people who come up during the interval and ask why I write songs, why I travel hundreds of miles to play for anyone who'll listen. It's a song about why a middle-class female from a comfortable background sings about working-class people and revolution. Let me play it for you, and then we'll take a break."

Patty plucks the banjo strings, the hollow sound an invitation. " 'Song of Myself.' "

*

I love those who labour, I sing of the farmers
And weavers and fishermen and miners as well;
Now all you who hear me, I pray you draw near me,
Before you grow weary, I'll sing of myself.
. . . . .
I join with the angry, I join with the hungry,
For long years of anguish the price will be paid.
To hate and to anger I am not a stranger,
I know there is danger and I am afraid.

For I fear the fate of the rebels and fighters
Who ransom the future with torture and pain.
As the trial comes near if I find I can dare it,
I'll willingly share it, no longer afraid.

For I've learned to be angry, I've learned to be lonely.
I've learned to be many, I've learned to be one.
I've earned all my friends, even foes will commend me.
I stand with the many, I am not alone.

In the presence of fighters I find a new peace,
In the company of workers replenish myself;
Of miners and weavers, of rebels and dreamers,
When I sing of my comrades, I sing of myself.[5]

✶

I watch the silent audience become a blur of scarves, coffee cups, beards, and glasses. They file by me immersed in conversation, and I feel as if I'm stealing something, noting their identity—age, ethnicity, countenance—as they pass. I write: "Male, sixties, talking to silver-haired lady with a cane . . . three giggly teenage girls . . . distracted man with a sleeping two-year-old slung over his shoulder . . . two fortyish women holding hands . . . all white."

Don slides into the seat next to mine. "Lots of conversation going on over by the restroom," he reports.

"OK, I'm going over there, then, to get some iced tea. Want anything?"

"No thanks. I'll just finish my coffee."

I make my way to the restroom, glad he's with me tonight. Don always notices the things I don't see, hears conversations I miss.

I smile when I see there's a line forming outside the restroom. It's usually easy to strike up a conversation or get into one when you're in line. I wait. "Patty's still pretty feisty," says the woman next to me. She looks at me, then at the other women in line. She's fortyish, wears a batik dress the colors of fire.

"It's not just feminism," the woman at the end of the line says, "it's classism." She's young, I'd say late twenties, and wears a plum beret pulled down over her ears. Lapis and onyx rings stretch a jagged crown on both hands.

"Socialism," the batiked woman corrects. "Patty is committed to the workers, the people who can't speak for themselves."

"I loved her song about baby boys," the lady in the beret says, changing the subject. "Why does this little piece of flesh get such a smile?" she asks, her question borrowing Patty's lyrics.

"Give him an inch and he'll take a mile," the fire-clad woman continues, supplying the last line of the song.

Laughter ricochets in the small hallway behind the stage.

*   *   *

As I return to my seat, the younger woman's comment pulls at my thoughts. "It's not just feminism, but classism." What does her observation imply? She was expecting a feminist performance, but why?

I unfold the March calendar and scan the description of Patty's music. In the boxed daily listing, her photo is accompanied by the caption "Legendary singer and composer—traditional and topical folk."

"Innocuous enough," I think, pulling open the tabloid to read the short biographies. Patty's reads: "This remarkable performer weaves a lifetime of advocacy into a narrative that involves her audience as a partner."

Advocacy seems a fitting word to describe Patty's dedication to issues of equality—for women, the handicapped, the poor—but perhaps it's vague enough to mislead . . . I sense a gap, a silence I can't quite identify.

Looking further, I notice a number of female performers, described as "key figures in the women's music movement," as "social and personal songstresses." This makes sense, March being Women's History Month. In fact, this event is mentioned in the biography for Resistive Voices, billed as celebrating women's history with "a concert of their pointed, often poignant original songs."

"Oh," I whisper, heart pounding as I realize what's missing. In February several performers were billed as participants in the Black History Month Series.

"No such series for March," I say, needing to share my discovery.

*   *   *

"Let me know if I can help," Sharon says to Brian as they emerge from the office.

"Ah, just the people I'm looking for," I say, hoping for an opportunity to talk with Brian. Since beginning this project, we've had only brief conversations. I'm anxious to get closer to him, hoping he'll open up a bit.

"What can we do for you?" Sharon asks, her smile luminous.

"I have a question about the March calendar." Brian, who is looking out over our heads, turns his attention to the conversation. "There are several women and women's music performers on the schedule."

"That's because it's Women's History Month," Brian says. "The calendar doesn't say it, but the bookings reflect it."

"Right. That's my question. Why a Black History series, but not a Women's History series?"

"Well, for the past few years we've had a grant to put the Black History series together, and February, which is Black History Month, is a way to showcase African-American artists. It's part of the grant."

"So you don't have a grant for women's music?"

"No, but it's our policy to not *ghettoize* women's music artists, or black artists for that matter," Brian explains, his words rushed. "We feature these artists all year long. We don't like to relegate them to a few weeks of bookings."

"So, featuring women's music artists doesn't mean this is a women's music venue, or at least that it doesn't want to be seen as such." I think these words, but remain silent.

"Then why all the women artists in March?" Sharon asks, anticipating my next question.

"Some might have requested bookings this month, but you'd have to ask Ricky about that." Brian and Sharon exchange a knowing glance. I'm confused.

"We didn't set out to pad the calendar with women," he says. "That's not the way we operate. No matter how much the artists or the patrons or the state Arts Council might like us to. Excuse me. Nice to see you, Stacy."

"You too. Thanks, Brian," I say to his back as he disappears into the office. I look at Sharon, not sure how to begin.

"I'll fill you in," she says. "Call me at home this week."

*   *   *

Patty sits on the edge of the stage, talking with those who surge toward her, just to talk or buy a CD—or "product," as we say in the States.

"Faith," she calls, recognizing her old friend amidst the faces of strangers. "How long has it been? Fifteen years?"

"Did you get my letter?" asks Faith. "I sent it about a couple of weeks ago, letting you know I'd be here tonight."

"No, but I'm so glad to see you. You look well."

"I'm an old woman. Been playing once in a blue moon. I can't even get arrested these days."

"We're slipping, I tell you," Patty says and laughs. "Seems like a lifetime ago we were banned from television, blacklisted."

"No more reds under the beds," Faith adds, chuckling. "Now they're after the greens in the trees. They don't realize it's the same people."

"Let's play something together," Patty suggests.

"I'd love it, but I didn't bring my guitar. Loan me yours?"

"Anything, Faith. Anything."

*   *   *

"I'd like to be a self-indulgent for a bit," Patty explains, beginning the second set. "And talk about what's happened to me over the last thirty-five years. It's funny how people go about getting what they want in life. Right now I'd like to bring up Faith Hemple, a dear friend, so we can play a tune together."

"Faith and Patty sing a song about old women and Winnebagos—funny," I write. "Then Patty sings songs about her children."

"And then, something incredible happened," Patty says after finishing the song. "My husband, my constant companion, died. For nearly six years I felt like half of me had been sliced off. And then I had the incredible fortune to fall in love again. I was giddy. And grateful.

"So I wrote six love songs. The sixth sets out the conjugal rules—something my mother said women shouldn't talk about. When I was growing up, and when my *mother* was growing up, women were told to lie back and think of England during sex, to think of all the soldiers they were producing. We weren't supposed to have any fun. Here's a subversive song I wrote, setting the rules."

I'm furiously trying to get down Patty's words. Most of the song passes while I recount bits of her story in my notebook. The song finishes with a flash of laughter and Patty begins another story.

"We've talked about love for a child and the earth and the desire that lovers share, but there are many kinds of love we haven't talked about. One kind we haven't talked about is a woman's love for her physical self." She plays a few bars of the song, then continues.

"I once read about a study where they showed women pictures of female bodies and asked, 'What shape are you most like?' Almost every woman chose a body shape *larger* than her own. The men in the same study almost always picked a body shape *smaller* than their own."

She swings the guitar away from her chest and extends her free arm, inviting us to look. She turns her own eyes on her body, letting her gaze travel from chest to toe. Then she looks up, looks out at the crowd and offers a brilliant smile. "I've tried to lose ten pounds most of my adult life . . . I must be trying to get into that smaller body." Laughter ripples through the audience.

"I wrote this song when I decided to keep my big body." She draws the guitar close once again and her voice, slight and tinny, soars above us: "My God, the things I did to you! . . . You were my enemy, you never were my friend."[6]

She plays the guitar furiously, then stops. "Switch to the key of F, which means maturity," she says. The audience titters, then quiets for her epigram. "My body, my friend, forgive me if you can, I love you just the way you are . . ."[7]

Applause lights up the room. "Thank you. Goodnight," Patty says and bows deeply.

Patty's song has my thoughts racing. I remember the Lina Michaels song, "Mama's Blues," the sound of her voice, the way her fingers lashed the strings.

I retreat to the women's restroom to write my thoughts. "Lina sings of her body in the third person, Patty the second, addressing 'it' directly. Both comment on the dualist nature of bodily perceptions in Western culture—the separation of the material, physical body from the spirit, soul, and mind. Susan Bordo[8] talks about the historicity of dual bodily experience . . . the body is viewed as:

alien, as not-self
confinement and limitation, a prison
enemy,
all that threatens our attempts at control
overwhelming
erupting
disrupting

"Bordo writes, 'The goal of humans, especially of women, is to free the mind from the body,' to 'become impervious to its distractions,' and most dangerous of all, to 'kill off its desires and hungers.'[9]

"In singing of their bodies," I write, "are Lina and Patty reclaiming their physicalness, their femininity? Uniting body and soul in performance?"

*　　　*　　　*

"Virginia," Brian says sternly, reaching behind her to grab the decaf pot. "I read your letter. You didn't have to do that." He sloshes coffee into a pottery mug.

"Yes I did."

"I hope this resolves the issue."

"I don't know if it does. I'm not sure everyone understands how uncomfortable we make it here for some people."

"We're doing everything we can."

"I don't think we are. You weren't here last night. Neither was Ricky. We had twelve people show up for the Celtic Singers. *Twelve* people. Yet we continue to book these kinds of groups and exclude others that might draw more of an audience."

"I wasn't here," Brian says, biting into a scone pilfered from the dessert counter. "But I deposited the door take. That group is part of Ricky's world music bookings. It's something the board has decided to pursue."

"Well maybe the board is out of touch with what's happening here. If they'd come in more. . . ."

"That's a problem," Brian interrupts.

"Last night Bob came in and walked right past the ticket desk. Josie's new and she hadn't met him yet, so she said, 'Sir, can I please see your ticket?' He turned to her and said, 'I'm the president of the board,' as if she's supposed to know this. I bet he hadn't been in here for two months!"

Brian issues a heavy sigh. "We're trying to improve things with the board. I've asked Sharon to come to the meetings, and we had the retreat."

"*Two* board members showed up to that retreat."

"Look, I want these problems resolved just as much as anybody . . . probably more so, but it doesn't happen overnight, and it doesn't happen by getting angry and shouting at each other." Brian's words come sharp and quick.

Virginia's eyes widen. "It doesn't happen by pretending these problems don't exist. I *cannot* do that, Brian."

"I don't expect you to," Brian says numbly. "Just give it some time." He takes his coffee into the office and latches the door behind him.

*   *   *

"Thank you," Patty says, returning to the stage for her encore. She wraps her guitar around her. "What would you like to hear?"

"Engineer" is shouted from all corners of the room.

"That's the problem when you write a catchy tune," Patty says. "You have to play it for the rest of your life. . . . Well, I suppose you won't let me out of here unless I play it. For those of you who don't know, I wrote this song in the '70s and it became an anthem of sorts for the women's movement in both Britain and the U.S. 'I'm Gonna Be an Engineer'."[10]

*

When I was a little girl, I wished I was a boy,
I tagged along behind the gang and wore my corduroys.
Everybody said I only did it to annoy
But I was gonna be an engineer.

Mama told me, 'Can't you be a lady?
Your duty is to make me the mother of a pearl.
Wait until you're older, dear, and maybe
You'll be glad that you're a girl.'

Dainty as a Dresden statue,
Gentle as a Jersey cow;
Smooth as silk, gives creamy milk,
Learn to coo, learn to moo,
That's what you do to be a lady now—

When I went to school I learned to write and how to read,
Some history, geography and home economy.
And typing is a skill that every girl is sure to need
To while away the extra time until the time to breed,
Then they had the nerve to say, 'What would you like to be?'
I says, 'I'm gonna be an engineer!'
No, you only need to learn to be a lady,
The duty isn't yours for to try and run the world.
An engineer could never have a baby!
Remember, dear, that you're a girl.

She's smart (for a woman).
I wonder how she got that way?
You get no choice, you get no voice,
Just stay mum, pretend you're dumb,
And that's how you come to be a lady today—

. . . .

Ah, but now that times are harder and my Jimmy's got the sack,
I went down to Vickers, they were glad to have me back,
But I'm a third class citizen (my wages tell me that)
And I'm a first-class engineer.

The boss says, 'We pay you as a lady,
You only got the job 'cause I can't afford a man.
And with you I keep the profits high as may be,
You're just a cheaper pair of hands.'

You got one fault: you're a woman.
You're not worth the equal pay.
A bitch or a tart, you're nothing but heart,
Shallow and vain, you got no brain,
You even go down the drain like a lady today—

Well, I listened to my mother and I joined a typing-pool;
I listened to my lover and I put him through his school;
But if I listen to the boss I'm just a bloody fool
And an underpaid engineer!
I been a sucker ever since I was a baby,
As a daughter, as a wife, as a mother and a 'dear.'
But I'll fight them as a woman, not a lady,
Fight them as an engineer!*

*

The applause rises and pulls the audience to its feet. Patty reaches her arms toward them. A smile plays across her face and she moves forward to the edge of the stage, disappearing into the hungry arms of her admirers.

*   *   *

---

* I'M GONNA BE AN ENGINEER
BY Peggy Seeger
© Copyright 1976, 1979 by STORMKING MUSIC INC.
All Rights Reserved Used by Permission

I feel guilty. It's been almost a week since I went to Patty's show, and I still haven't written my fieldnotes. In fact, I haven't written *any* fieldnotes since my disappointing discussion of women's music.

"You had to do some research first," I say to an empty office. "Now you're ready," I add, unconvinced.

Fieldnotes ....

3.9.96
The Club, 8:30–11:00 p.m.

Patty Sanders is an overtly political performer, addressing not only women's issues, but concerns including the environment, labor, health, rights of the disabled. From the start, I felt the performance would provide a nice contrast to the other shows I've seen, as well as some good musical material. And I think I got some great stuff—the woman commenting that "it's not just feminism, but classism," and our almost guilty pleasure in reliving her lyrics, "give him an inch and he'll take a mile."

Patty's moving performance of "I'm Gonna Be an Engineer" seemed to be the highlight of the evening for the audience, but for me, her song "Getting It Right" was the most memorable experience. I was struck by the similarities between this performance and Lina Michaels' song "Mama's Blues." Both late in the show, almost afterthoughts, these songs were offered as glimpses into the performer's life, woman's experience. Let's see. . . .

Bordo's writing about women's relationships with their bodies provides an interesting starting point: the Western notion of the body as separate from mind and soul, as apart from the self, as "undermining the best efforts of that self" (5). We perceive the physical self as alien, a vessel of confinement, as enemy and threat to psychological control. Calling on Foucault's concept of "docile bodies," Bordo argues that women desire and create "bodies whose forces and energies are habituated to external regulation, subjection, transformation, improvement. . . . Through these disciplines, we continue to memorize on our bodies the feel and conviction of lack, of insufficiency, of never being good enough" (166).

Both Lina and Patty sing of the inadequacy they feel in, and about, their bodies. Lina's song depicts an almost debilitating deficiency that physically weakens the woman, silences her: "There are days when every bone in her body is achin'/When she feels like everyone hates her/And she cannot speak/And she sees herself as ugly/And unworthy of any love." And Patty clearly perceives her body as the *enemy*: "My God, the things I did to you/you were my enemy, you never were my friend."

Foucault's notion of self-surveillance and the power of self-coercion is also evident in these songs. In "The Eye of Power" he writes:

> ...there is no need for arms, physical violence, material constraints. Just a gaze. An inspecting gaze, a gaze which each individual under its weight will end by interiorising to the point that he is his own overseer, each individual thus exercising this surveillance over, and against himself (155).

Adopting a powerful, inspecting gaze, Lina sings, "Now she's lookin' at her body in the mirror/And she's cryin' 'cause her waist/Is not as tiny as before the baby/And she feels like the world is at an end/And she thinks nobody is every gonna/Want her body again." The woman in Lina's song is clearly her own "overseer," deciding *against* herself, her body, undermining her *self*.

Thus, in addition to my previous observation that Lina the performer may be under surveillance by the bearded man in the audience, I see that Lina not only observes and monitors herself, but also makes this self-surveillance *visible* to the audience through her song. What is accomplished is not merely a reflection of *audience-performer* surveillance, but instead, a more kaleidoscopic refraction of *social* surveillance of women—surveillance by men, but also by women. These multiple gazes, audience–performer, male–female, female–female, and female–self–these surveillances—are leveled, felt, inscribed rejected, and altered in performance.

I'm reminded of Laurel Richardson's characterization of post-modern writing (which has strong ties to performance) as not sub-scribing to the notion of triangulation, but rather, *crystallization*. Unlike the triangle, "Crystals are prisms that reflect externalities and refract within themselves" ("Writing" 522). Through crystal-lization, we "feel how there is no single truth, we see how texts validate themselves; and crystallization provides us with a deep-ened, complex, thoroughly partial, understanding" (522). In the performance of these songs, I see the kaleidoscopic *crystallization* of myriad gazes and performances of sexuality, gender, desire, identity, artistry.

It's also interesting that the woman in Lina's song is disgusted by the look of her *maternal* body, resisting this "natural" form in favor of a more girlish figure—one not yet capable of bearing children. Bordo makes some insightful comments about this dis-position, arguing that desiring and working to achieve a girlish look may symbolize "liberation from a domestic, reproductive destiny" (206). By controlling their "desires" (hungering, sexual, maternal), women may achieve this liberation.

However, perpetuation of the "tightly managed body" as the contemporary ideal of female attractiveness may also work to sus-tain an even greater level of self-surveillance and self-correction, as the steady increase of eating disorders would indicate (see Bordo).

Indeed, Lina's song seems to say that the woman's failure to manage her body—to achieve the feminine ideal—means she will lose all that was once hers: her relationship, her voice. The song ends with the man, unable to understand the woman's "state of mind," being comforted by the "young girls": "And he wonders what she wants from him/And he's sittin' drinkin' coffee at the breakfast stand/And he tells the waitress that it's lonely at home/And all the young girls take pity on him." Here, the woman's relationship—the relationship through which she has defined her body, her self—is in jeopardy because her body no longer conforms to an ephemeral, yet *real*, vision of her physical presence. And she is unable to speak about the threat she feels.

The self-surveillance of which Lina and Patty sing may also illustrate the male-as-norm and heterosexual-as-norm (following Langellier, Carter, and Hantzis) expectation in performance, but their songs transcend the margins of performance to comment on contemporary culture. Bordo notes that current cultural representations of femininity and beauty work both to *"homogenize"* (that is, eradicate gender and sexuality differences) and to *"normalize"* maleness and heterosexuality. Thus, predominant cultural representations of gender and sexual orientation "function as models against which the self continually measures, judges, and 'disciplines' and 'corrects' itself" (25). In the stare of surveillance, woman's body becomes an object—separate from, yet inextricably tied to—a culturally and physically *constructed* self.

The performance of "Mama's Blues," in particular, may evidence the male- and heterosexual-as-norm expectations *through* its reflexive depiction of the feminine model of bodily "discipline" and "correction." The woman in the song reflects on her state of mind and identity as it is *mis*understood by the man in her life: "And he looks at her like she's crazy/And he does not understand/He doesn't think she looks much different/Or much fatter than before/Yeah, she seems to look the same to him/And she's sad that he can't relate to her state of mind."

The feelings conveyed in the song may be testimony to the efficacy of male, heterosexual norms, characterized by Anne Marie Hunter as lack of privacy for women, self-imposed surveillance, and the normalization of a publicly performed persona that is always available to meet the needs of others (those more powerful) in her life—men, children, even other women (10–11). Further, the woman in the song self-corrects and disciplines her body and her self based on male, heterosexual perception and expectation of a thin female body. The woman understands more about the predicament of her gender identity—her unattractiveness and failure to live up to the male ideal—than the man in the song. It is the *woman* who is aware of her body's ability to measure up to—to perform—the culturally constructed physical norm of a slender, tight, absolutely controlled body, unaltered by mother-hood, age, weakness.

At the same time, "Mama's Blues" testifies to an internal iden-tity not constructed or reflected in the male gaze, a self marked off from the "public" persona of woman. And within this "private" self, there is possibility: possibility capable of altering the physical self in empowering and resistive ways. As Bordo reminds us, "Modern power-relations are thus unstable, resistance is perpet-ual and hegemony precarious" (28).

This discussion raises questions about what constitutes these male/female, masculine/feminine, and heterosexual/homosexual power differentials. Performance provides a means of under-standing these multifaceted distinctions without enlisting an essentialist logic that collapses the multiple positions and subjec-tivities of women into a monolithic experience. Beginning in *Gen-der Trouble*, Judith Butler develops an extensive critique of the notion that men and women possess gendered identities that form a "core" or an "interior" gendered self. Rather, she proposes that gender is created and inscribed on and through our bodies in social interaction—in *performance*. She writes, "gender proves to be performative—that is, constituting the identity it is purported to be. In this sense, gender is always a doing, though not a doing by a subject who might be said to preexist the deed" (25). Further, gendered performance is imbricated within structures of racial and class oppression. Indeed, race and class become the site from which gender identity is articulated (*Bodies That Matter* 130).

Within the notion of an "interior and organizing gender core" lies the *presupposition* and naturalization of male, heterosexual identities (Butler, *Gender Trouble* 136). Butler notes that this is a *fantasy* "instituted and inscribed on the surface of bodies" through performance (136). And Bordo writes of the constitutive efficacy of this fantasy in Western culture: "That illusion, moreover . . . effec-tively protects the institution of reproductive heterosexuality from scrutiny and critique as an institution, continually regulating rather than merely reflecting our sexuality" (290).

Thus, characterizing gender identity as performative opens up the possibility for multiple perceptions of the body and gender. Individuals are able to isolate, reflect, question, and adopt various gender "configurations" in performance, and in turn, audiences can engage in equally complex, gendered interpretations. And as Susan McClary suggests, music plays a central role in this performative efficacy:

> ...music is foremost among cultural "technologies of the body," . . . it is a site where we learn how to experience socially mediated patterns of kinetic energy, being in time, emotions, desire, pleasure, and much more. . . . [M]usic thus provides a terrain where competing notions of the body (and also the self, ideals of social interaction, feelings, and so on) vie for attention and influence (445).

Women's music performances at The Club seem to illustrate gender identity and competing notions of the body in all of their complexity. From the rhetoric surrounding the performance (calendar write-ups, photos, flyers), the physical appearance and actions of the performer, and the lyrics and stories presented, to the look and behavior of the audience, questions arise about the gendered nature of performance. Is the performer characterized as a "women's music" artist? Does she sing about women's issues? Does she perform, in lyric and body, her sexuality? Is this performance of sexuality direct or indirect? Do audience members come because of the perceived topical nature of the performance? Do they speak of and embody their sexuality? Are these performances direct or indirect? And, just as important, who is absent from these performances—women and men of color, as Virginia asserts? People outside of the middle-class? How does women's music intersect with issues surrounding race and class?

Lina Michaels', Elaine Baker's, and Cheryl Wheeler's performances provide interesting responses to these questions. While billed as a "women's blues" artist (which I've taken to mean a particular genre of women's music), and while openly addressing women's issues, Lina is also clear about her heterosexual orientation. Yet, I could argue (and the letter from Marcus Taylor would support this assertion) that there were many lesbian couples in the audience, creating potential personal, gendered meanings, pleasures, and performances from the messages in Lina's music.

Conversely, Elaine Baker and Cheryl Wheeler were not billed as women's music artists, but they clearly addressed women's issues, as well as lesbian themes, in their songs. And the audience wasn't appreciably different from those attending Lina Michaels' show. What seems to be happening is both blind, blatant misunderstanding and sophisticated, tacit understanding of the atmosphere and content of these shows. These various understandings give rise to a multiplicity of performances and perceptions that vary according to gender identity. Of course, these various performances seem to occur, as Virginia notes, within a predominately white, middle-class environment and discourse, which limits their accessibility and appeal to women of other classes and colors. Indeed, this has long been an assertion against women's music in general, which, in some settings, serves to divide women along racial and class lines (Eder, Staggenborg, and Sudderth 501).

Thus, for the predominately white audience and women's music performers presented at The Club, multiple perceptions and interpretations give rise to the *possibility* of performing alternative gender identities "outside the restricting frames of masculinist domination and compulsory heterosexuality" (Butler, *Gender Trouble* 141). For these women, possibility lives in performance.

But "What kind of gender performance will enact and reveal the performativity of gender itself in a way that destabilizes the naturalized categories of identity and desire?" (Butler, *Gender Trouble* 139). It is in the moment of surveillance and the policing of gendered performance that the possibility for transcending socially constructed identities emerges. As I noted previously, "bodies of women, bodies of color, bodies that 'do not perform their genders correctly' are performance sights that challenge the socially constructed ways of looking" (Bell 115). This is possible because gender is constituted in performance, and in performance, "productive 'trouble' " might be made for "entrenched assumptions about what is 'natural and what is 'unnatural' " (Bordo 290), at least for the white women present. And perhaps these performers, audiences, and members might begin to make "productive trouble" for the racial inequities in The Club's bookings and audience composition, making "bodies of color" a more frequent and disruptive performance sight.

Nonetheless, in these performances, artists and audience members alike are able to make "trouble" for mainstream assumptions about gender identity and sexuality. So even though a performer might be referred to as "some lesbian," and members might complain about the composition of audiences and topical nature of the music—also performances that may work to reaffirm established assumptions about what is natural and what is not— others can challenge these perceptions and experience an alternative, subversive, resistant performance. The question, then, is how might the performances at The Club be categorized? As reaffirming? resistive? recuperative? all three? both/and? How do these performances reflect and refract multiple perceptions and experiences? How are multiple gazes and performances of sex, gender, desire, and artistry crystallized in women's music performances?

"Ah, Stacy . . . ," a deep male voice sounds in my head. "Must these performances be typed? Categorized?"

I am stunned. "Huh?"

"You seem to accept unquestioningly the aim of categorization."

"Who *are* you?"

"Art."

"*Art Bochner?*" I ask, amazed.

"Yep. Carolyn is here too."

"Hi, Stacy," a woman says.

"*Carolyn Ellis?*"

"You evoked us in your last set of fieldnotes, remember?" Art asks.

"Sure, but . . ."

"So," he begins, "we're wondering why you've backed away from the postmodern sensibility and evocative text you were after twenty-five pages back. Why you're so determined to categorize women's music performances. The strength of this work lies in the mystery and complexity of your experiences, as well as the difficulty you find in making categorizations."

I nod. "You're right," I say, "but I feel as if I'm spinning my wheels. As if I can't get any closure on this."

"If you're after an open text, why is closure important?" Carolyn asks.

"Maybe it's not."

Art clears his throat. "Do you believe that you can get outside of your own experience and subjectivity—or that of your informants—in this work?"

"No," I say, certain of only this.

"Then why expend so much effort trying to escape *language*?"[11] Carolyn interjects. "Think about that," she says, and then their voices are gone.

An open text. One that reveals the complexity and richness of women's music performances. One that makes room not only for my interpretations—my language— but also for the voices of scholars, performers, members of The Club, and audiences.

A performative text. One that celebrates language as it evokes and *crystallizes* the thoughts and feelings of my ethnographic experience. Richardson reminds me that "crystallization provides us with a deepened, complex, thoroughly partial, understanding of the topic. Paradoxically, we know more and doubt what we know" ("Writing" 522). She encourages the writer who adopts a postmodern sensibility:

> Postmodern sociologists have unique opportunities to fulfill the promise of the sociological imagination. They can write the lives

of individuals, groups, and collectives, grounding social theory in people's experiences and celebrating diversity and multiplicity . . . postmodernism celebrates multiplicity of method and multiple sites of contestation. Postmodernism can expand our understanding of what constitutes social theory, who can do it, and how it might be represented ("Postmodern Social Theory" 177).

An open, performative text. One that allows me to fully explore my ethnographic experiences . . . and my self. Rhythm. Poetry. Richardson says poetry creates "rhythms, silences, spaces, breath points, alliterations, meter, cadence, assonance, rhyme, and off-rhyme" that "engage the listener's body, even when the mind resists and denies it" ("Writing" 522).

Perhaps poetry will enable me to more vividly evoke women's music performances, to record how women's bodies, genders, sexualities, and musics are performed at The Club. These performances—these events—are more poetic than scientific. More lyric than fieldnotes. Perhaps poetry opens the text to . . . experience. Perhaps poetry brings to life a performative presence. . . .

> Flourish strings and voices rise
> Overseer, actor, emancipator,
> Artist, woman, prisoner, lover
> Cheek-to-cheek, corpulent footsteps
> Join voices weaving golden skeins
> Singer and dancer waver, inside-out
>
> Well-trained skeptics, disavowing scowls
> Postmodern funhouse mirrors cleave authenticity
> Thespians costume gender identity
> Voices raised, bodies bared in dedication
> Character and gender dance and sing
> Of deep knowing, complex half-truths

> Writer, detective, woman struggles
> To pen the kaleidoscope play
> To paint fleeting harmony, dizzy change
> To stir milk's smooth surface
> To verse tide pools of resistance
> Learns to love
> Learns to know more and doubt that

. . . .

I feel exhilarated. My skin tingles with a satisfaction I have not felt in months—the contentment of making something complex, something mysterious, come alive in words. Tracing women's multiple, conflicting, refracting identities, and relationships . . . the intricate weave of these identities, relationships in postmodern performance—fabrics that are not worn, but inscribed on the body . . . the epiphany and frustration of my work.

The pleasure melts away as I read my awkward words. "You can't write a coherent set of fieldnotes, let alone a scholarly essay." I announce out loud. "And you're no poet."

Don interrupts my criticism with a soft knock at the office door. "You want to take a break, get something to eat?"

"I'm starving," I say. "Just let me save this." Forgetting my reservations, I spare the poem certain obliteration, save it to disk, and silence the computer's insistent hum.

Notes

1. Nicole Broussard, quoted in Karen Gould, "Setting Words Free: Feminist Writing in Quebec," *Signs* 6.4 (1976): 629.
2. Peggy Seeger, "I'm Gonna Be an Engineer," rec., *Peggy Seeger, The Folkways Years 1955–1992: Songs of Love and Politics,* Smithsonian/Folkways, 1992.
3. Susan McClary, "Same As It Ever Was: Youth Culture and Music," *Rock She Wrote: Women Write About Rock, Pop, and Rap,* ed. Evelyn McDonnell and Ann Powers (New York: Delta, 1995), 444.
4. Barbara Engh, "Loving It: Music and Criticism in Roland Barthes," *Musicology and Difference: Gender and Sexuality in Musical Scholarship,* ed. Ruth A. Solie (Berkeley: University of California Press, 1993), 74.
5. Seeger, "Song of Myself," rec., *Peggy Seeger, The Folkways Years 1955–1992: Songs of Love and Politics,* Smithsonian/Folkways, 1992.
6. Seeger and Irene Scott, "Getting It Right," rec., *Almost Commercially Viable: No Spring Chickens,* Golden Egg Productions, 1991.
7. Seeger, "Getting It Right," rec., *Peggy Seeger, The Folkways Years 1955–1992: Songs of Love and Politics,* Smithsonian/Folkways, 1992.
8. Susan Bordo, *Unbearable Weight: Feminism, Western Culture, and the Body* (Berkeley: University of California Press, 1993), 144–45. The author describes four central features of Cartesian dualism: First, that the body is *alien*, "the not self, the not-me." Second, the body is "experienced as *confinement and limitation.*" Third, the body is "*the enemy* . . . the source of obscurity and confusion in our thinking." Fourth, the body is "the locus of *all that threatens our attempts at control.*"
9. Bordo, 145.
10. Arthur P. Bochner and Carolyn Ellis, "Talking Over Ethnography," *Composing Ethnography: Alternative Forms of Qualitative Writing,* ed. Carolyn Ellis and Arthur P. Bochner (Walnut Creek, Calif.: AltaMira Press, 1996), 20. The authors assert, "when we say ethnographers can't stand above or outside language, we mean that the world as we 'know' it cannot be separated from the language we use to explain, understand, or describe it" (20).

Evocative writing touches us where we live, in our bodies. Through it we can experience the self-reflexive and transformational process of self-creation.

Laurel Richardson, "Writing: A Method of Inquiry"[1]

•

•

•

•

•

Making it through the summer of ethnography means working even when fatigued, heat-exhausted, and weary. . . . As relationships build and fatigue grows, the potential for conflict and confrontation of personal biases increases. . . . The irony is that it is the conflict which begins to arise here which is integral to obtaining true understanding of another culture.

M. Cristina Gonzalez, *The Four Seasons of Ethnography*[2]

•

•

•

•

•

She's going to figure out what's wrong with us and then write a book about it.

Brian, business manager of The Club

•

•

•

•

•

5

The Toyota of Ethnography

I'M TIRED. And hungry. I don't want to be here tonight. This project has me frayed at the edges, and yet I feel guilty about not spending more time here. I've seen so much, yet know so little. Part of me thinks that experiencing more will help me emerge from this difficult place; another cautions that I need time away.

"You're here," I remind myself, deciding to make the most of my visit. I think of Mitchell and feel a pang of regret. We'd planned to meet for an interview this afternoon, but we couldn't find a time that worked for both of us. I'd wanted to talk to him about the early days at The Club, to try to piece together the history of the organization. When it was clear we couldn't make our schedules meet, I'd fired off my questions via e-mail.

. . . .

Subj: Early Days at The Club
Date: 20 March 1996
From: stacyhj@aol.com
To: 34567.3421@compuserve.com

Mitchell: No problem about the interview. I'll go ahead
and send you the questions I wanted to ask. Feel free to
respond via e-mail. Can you describe the social scene in
the Bay Area when you first became involved with The
Club? Can you describe the early days at The Club—
memorable performances, the interests of the artists
and audiences? What role did women play in the organization in those days? Were there women's music performances then?

. . . .

Mitchell's reply made me feel demanding and impatient. I'd
placed the burden of my interests on him, and he'd let me know it.

. . . .

Subj: Early Days at The Club
Date: 21 March 1996
From: 34567.3421@compuserve.com
To: stacyhj@aol.com

Stacy: Your questions are awfully inclusive, but I'll be
thinking along those lines. However, I'm not prepared to
develop an essay on the demography of the Bay Area folk
scene in the late '60s, nor am I qualified to give a considered overview of women's music at any period. What I
can offer is vague memories of how I perceived the alternative music field at that time. Let me know. Mitchell

. . . .

I felt ashamed and anxious at the same time. My deadline for com-
pleting the project was approaching at an alarming rate, and I needed
Mitchell's help to finish my work. I'd have to set things right with him.

*   *   *

"I'm so pleased to be introducing tonight's show, which had its making more than three years ago in a Tucson hotel room," Ricky says into the mike, surveying the audience. I'm surprised to hear him introducing the performers. Sharon or one of the other night managers usually does the introductions.

"That night I had the great pleasure to witness the meeting of Chrissy and Kathy, two of folk music's most beautiful voices. They stayed up until dawn playing, and the realization they were on to something special was a thrill to witness. *Walkin' the Floor*, the release of which we're celebrating, is a testament to the magical chemistry these two wonderful singers have—magic that you'll witness tonight on our stage." The crowd interrupts Ricky with a spattering of applause. "It is my great pleasure to introduce Chrissy Lovell, Kathy Campbell, and James Stringer."

"Who's James Stringer?" I write, a faint memory tugging at me. I remember as soon as the performers take the stage. James and Chrissy are married and have collaborated on several traditional folk music albums. He moves to a far corner of the stage and turns toward the singers, clearly taking a secondary role.

Chrissy and Kathy are dressed in velvet—Kathy wears black leggings and an oversized shirt, Chrissy a flowing scarlet dress. The stage lights shine through onyx hair, illuminating their faces.

"Good evening," Kathy says. "We should've asked Ricky to put a box of tissues on each table."

"If you've heard the album, you'll know why," Chrissy interjects.

"In Austin, the best music in the area is played at an event called Bummer Night," Kathy continues. "You can do fifty sad songs in a row and nobody'll bust you."

"And tonight is Bummer Night at The Club," Chrissy says. "This first song is about good love gone bad."

I write in my notebook: "Chrissy and Kathy sing several sad songs—most of them even have 'Sad' in the title."

Their style is decidedly different from that of the other performers I've seen recently—more country influences, in terms of both the sound and the lyrics. I think about Patty Sanders' show, about how political she was, and the wide range of topics she covered.

A cloud of disappointment creeps into my notes. "Is this *women's* music? The show doesn't have the feel of the others, although I can't quite put my finger on why. The audience seems the same—mostly white, maybe a few more men than usual. Maybe it's me. Maybe I'm just losing energy, enthusiasm?"

My notes dwindle to quick notations of song titles and bits of the polite conversation Chrissy and Kathy make between songs. I shift in my seat, bored with their radiant harmonies and hopeful that something will happen during the intermission—something to make my trip worthwhile.

*   *   *

"Hi!" I say when faced with Ricky. An overly exuberant welcome, but I want to talk to him, and he looks as if he's headed somewhere past me. Graying and stocky, Ricky looks like my high school band teacher.

"How's it goin'?" he asks politely.

"Great. I'm really enjoying the show," I lie. "I'm glad I ran into you. I have a question."

"Sure."

"I'm curious about the March calendar. I noticed that while you have several women performers on the schedule, you don't mention Women's History Month." I want to hear Ricky's version and compare it to what Brian said.

"Very astute, you noticing that." Ricky pulls at his beard. "Fact is, we talked about it, but I put the calendar together in a hurry because I was leaving town. We should've done something, but we just ran out of time."

"Well, I *did* see a note in one of the descriptions you wrote," I offer.

"Yeah, like I said, we talked about it, probably should've done something, although. . . ."

"Hmm?"

"The scheduling just kind of worked out that way," he says, then purses his lips. "We have women performers year-round."

"Did anyone request bookings in March?"

"No, not really. It just worked out that way. Like Chrissy and Kathy. Just worked out that the album was released this month. I don't know if you heard my introduction, but I was there when they met," he says, standing a bit taller.

"That must've been incredible."

"It was a wonderful night," he says, looking past me. "I see Kathy. Will you excuse me?"

"Sure. Thanks, Ricky."

I walk into the lobby, recognizing many people on the way. Here's Chrissy and James, standing in a circle of two other women and a man. They sing a hushed, complex harmony.

There's the tall, wiry couple with glasses—they look strikingly similar, although she's got longer hair. They've been at almost every performance I've attended at The Club, their two small children routinely snuggled together on the threadbare lobby couch by the end of the evening.

And the man in the black leather jacket and thick-framed glasses leans up against a wall. Seems I always sit near him, his bulky boots keeping time, eyelids fluttering to the music.

I sit in a mud-colored chair in the lobby and record my talk with Ricky. A recent phone conversation with Sharon had made me curious. She'd told me about the conflicts between Brian and Ricky over bookings, about Brian's frustration with not being responsible for the entire operation. Because of the tension Sharon described, I'd expected Ricky's account of writing the March calendar to be different than Brian's, evidence of the rift between them. Ricky's ideas about the calendar—that they intended to celebrate the occasion, that they should've done so—are different from Brian's: no ghettoizing women, no deliberate decision not to publicize Women's History Month.

But the streams of their rhetoric ultimately *do* have confluence. They agree The Club did not set out to book a number of women's music artists for March. And both remind me that women performers comprise a significant number of the acts booked to perform each year. Maybe the tension between them isn't as great as I thought? Or about what I thought it was about? Or wanted it to be about?

*   *   *

"Stacy . . . Stacy?" Brian's voice stirs me from my notebook.

I look up. "Oh, Brian. Hi."

"I want to introduce you to Ron Gardner. He teaches music history at St. Luke's College."

My hand is lost in his enormous grip. "Hi, Ron."

He offers a shy grin. "Hi."

"You and Stacy are the academics who're going to make The Club famous," Brian says.

"Oh yeah?" I joke. "What are you working on, Ron?"

"I'm teaching a course on the history of country music. I send my students here to see country performers. And I've done extensive interviews with Brian, here, and Mitchell Smith. Got them on audio tape."

"Stacy might want to hear those tapes," Brian interrupts.

"I do!"

"I'll get them over to Brian next week."

"Stacy's also done several interviews with Club musicians and employees," Brian continues. "How many hours of tape do you have?"

"I don't know. About twenty, twenty-five, I guess."

"She's got some great stuff," Brian says proudly, surprising me. "We can't wait until she's finished."

"What are you doing?" Ron asks, turning to me.

"I'm studying the communication and culture of the organization. Actually, I'm focusing on women's music performances. . . ." I stop, hoping I won't have to explain the connection between the two. I'm not sure I *can.*

"She's going to figure out what's wrong with us," Brian teases.

"That would take too long," I say, playing along.

"Then you'll have to write a book about it."

Ron reaches into his back pocket, removes his wallet and flips it open. He slides a business card out from behind a twenty-dollar bill and offers it to me. "Here's my card. My e-mail address is included. Do you have e-mail?"

"Yeah," I say, then nudge Brian. "I'll send you a message and we can trade secrets about this guy."

The lights blink twice, and I'm anxious to get back to my seat. "Nice to meet you, Ron. I'll be in touch."

We shake hands and I make my way back into the main room. I think of Brian's words and feel a tightness in my stomach. I'm proud that he wanted to introduce me to Ron, and pleased he has great expectations for my project. And I'm grateful to the people who've made me feel at home here the past two years. But I'm worried about what they expect from me. I want to give something back to them, but I'm not sure what. Do they want some sort of organizational history? A report on their communication processes—or problems? I'm sure they don't want the musings of a frustrated, sometime writer. An analysis of women's music. The variously fuzzy, critical, romantic picture I've painted. What good would it be to them? How would *I* even know what's good for them?

* * *

Chrissy and Kathy continue the second set with more of their trademark "sad tunes." They focus on lost love—men hurting women: "So Sad," "Childish Love," and "Still Blue," and women who'll do anything to get their men back: "I'll Take the Blame," and "Sad But True."[3]

I wonder about the contrasts between tonight's music and that played during other shows I've seen. Besides the obvious lack of political topics, these songs speak of different types of people, of different kinds of women. Where Lina, Elaine, Cheryl, and Patty sing of ardent women playing strong, if difficult, roles in relationships, Chrissy and Kathy's music is infused with the more traditional "if you leave me, I will surely die syndrome."[4]

And the other performances seemed somehow more personal than those in tonight's show. Cynthia Lont[5] characterizes women's music performers as more willing to make a connection with their audiences, more willing to appear vulnerable, and as expecting audiences to evaluate their work based on both lyrical content *and* musical artistry.

But these expectations seem to be the "norm" for most, if not all, Club performances. Many artists, Club employees, and audience members have spoken to me about the intimacy of the venue, the attentiveness of the listeners, the personal feel of the performances. Performers say, "I'm more excited, and nervous at the same time, because my peers are in the audience," and "It's so quiet in here you feel like you're in church."

I feel that closeness and rapture tonight, but it's opaque; a thin veil of reserve separates me. Maybe women's music performances here are even more immediate? Perhaps an even greater exchange takes place between audience and performer?

*　　*　　*

"So they spend the whole film talking about where to get good sushi," the thin man says, his tiny mustache so close to the woman it brushes her face.

"That's it," the woman says with an English accent. She's swaddled in an scarf that covers her head and most of her body. "That's all that happens the whole time. No, I take that back. They talk about the fact that sushi's all they're talking about. It's bloody boring."

"That's the point," the man says, looking annoyed. "It's antithetical. Ahistorical. It's *postmodern*."

"Postmodern!" the woman whines, then pulls away. "That says everything. And nothing."

I give a quick laugh, more movement than sound, and think of John Rajchman's description of postmodern theory in all its "ahistoricity" and "antitheticalness": it's "like the Toyota of thought: produced and assembled in several different locations and then sold everywhere."[6]

I also think about the postmodern narrative I'm writing—no, *want* to be writing. Laurel Richardson tells me writing should reflect the partiality and particularity of the situation. She says that no matter how much I might try to suppress it, my *self* will be present in my writing. Well, that's a lie. Actually, parts of myself must be present in the writing, because just as in situations and cultures and contexts, something of the self is always masked, repressed. She says I must try to tell and retell the story. That I shouldn't worry about "getting it right," only about "getting it."[7]

Ihab Hassan agrees and disagrees with Laurel. He says postmodern literature is:

play	*not*	*purpose*
process/performance/happening	*not*	*art object/finished work*
change	*not*	*design*
combination	*not*	*selection*
desire	*not*	*symptom*
indeterminacy	*not*	*determinacy*[8]

Ihab's litany and Laurel's encouragement make me feel confident and lost. Where does "both/and" reside in Ihab's neat dichotomies? Am I reading between the lines? Am I writing partiality and particularity? Is it processual, performative? Am I writing the story of The Club and of myself? Is my work the product of desire and not the symptom of my academic training? Am I *getting* it?

You tell me.

*   *   *

I push my way through the crowd huddled around a table spread with Chrissy's and Kathy's CDs and cassettes, holding my purchase close.

"Just in case," I'd thought, writing the check. But I knew that, once home, I wouldn't want to tear the plastic off right away, to search eagerly for the liner notes, in hopes that the lyrics were preserved for me. But perhaps listening to Chrissy and Kathy sing of loss as I write of their performance will help me see their connection to the others, help me understand my ambivalence. I stop and swallow hard. Just a few feet away, talking to Brian, stands Mitchell. Dread flushes my face. Guilt propels me toward him.

We make eye contact before I get to where he and Brian are standing. He lifts his chin, beckoning me.

"Hi, Mitchell," I say sheepishly.

"Hello. Our play finished early, so Gina and I thought we'd catch the end of Chrissy's and Kathy's show. You enjoy it?"

"Sure."

"I need to settle up with the ladies," Brian says, slapping Mitchell on the back, then turning his gaze on me. "I'll let you know when those tapes of Ron's come in."

"Thanks, Brian," I say as he walks away, unsure how to address Mitchell now that we're alone.

"Sorry we couldn't get together this afternoon," he begins.

"Mitchell. . . ."

"And if I sounded terse in my e-mail, I apologize."

"No, Mitchell, you were right. I shouldn't expect you to give me a short course in Bay Area folk history."

"You didn't ask me to," says Mitchell, smiling now.

"You've been so helpful to me, I've just come to *rely* on you."

He places a fatherly hand on my shoulder. "I'm glad to help. It wasn't so long ago I was in school. It's just that I'm really busy with playing and the business, and Gina's very demanding of my time on the weekends."

"I understand," I say, eager to have this resolved. "Why don't we leave it at this: If you have any stories from those days that stand out for you, e-mail them to me."

"It's a deal. I need to catch up with Gina, so I'll say goodnight."

"Goodnight, Mitchell. Thanks."

I breathe deep and walk out into the cool darkness. As I stand in front of my battered imported car trying to fit the key into the lock, I laugh.

"You're writing 'The Toyota of Ethnography'!" I yell into the night.

*   *   *

"Did you write up your fieldnotes for last weekend's show?" Don asks later, at home, as we're about to crawl into bed for the night.

"No."

"Why not?"

"I'm waiting until I'm ready to know,"[9] I say.

Notes

1. Laurel Richardson, "Writing: A Method of Inquiry," *Handbook of Qualitative Research*, ed. Norman K. Denzin and Yvonna S. Lincoln (Thousand Oaks, Calif.: Sage, 1994), 521.

2. M. Cristina Gonzalez, *The Four Seasons of Ethnography* (unpublished manuscript, 1996), 25–26.

3. Titles from Kate Brislin and Katy Moffatt, *Sleepless Nights*, rec., Rounder, 1996.

4. Cynthia M. Lont, "Between Rock and a Hard Place: A Model of Subcultural Persistence and Women's Music," diss., University of Iowa, 1984, 93. A phrase used by Lont to describe the depiction of women in popular music.

5. Lont, 94.

6. John Rajchman, "Postmodernism in a Nominalist Frame: The Emergence and Diffusion of a Cultural Category," *Flash Art* 137 (1987): 51.

7. Richardson, 521. She writes, "Postmodernism claims that writing is always partial, local, and situational, and that our Self is always present, no matter how much we try to suppress it—but only partially present, for in our writing we repress parts of ourselves too. Working from that premise, we are freed to write material in a variety of ways: to tell and retell. There is no such thing as 'getting it right,' only 'getting it' differently contoured and nuanced."

8. Ihab Hassan, *The Dismemberment of Orpheus: Toward a Postmodern Literature* (New York: Oxford University Press, 1982), 267–68. This list is derived from Hassan's table of the opposing terms that apply to "postmodernism" and "modernism."

9. Gonzalez, 28. The author writes that "the insight of wisdom into a culture requires tenacity and willingness to wait until one is ready to 'know.' And even then, 'knowing' is tentative."

Now, women forget all those things they don't want to remember, and remember everything they don't want to forget. The dream is the truth.

Zora Neale Hurston, *Their Eyes Were Watching God*[1]

I'm a feminist singer and spokeswoman. Mine is a politics as if everyone mattered.

Spoken during a performance at The Club

I seem to have an awful lot of people inside me.

Edith Evans, cited in *The Harper Book of Quotations*[2]

6

Don't You

"IT'S SO GOOD to see you, Hannah," Emily says, then stuffs a spoonful of tabouli into her mouth. "I can't believe it's been almost a year since I saw my baby sister," she mumbles.

"It's been a long time since I've been in the Bay Area," Hannah replies. "Or since I've been to a show at The Club. I'm glad Robert could stay with the kids."

"Is he having any luck finding work in San Francisco?"

"Not really. I'm sort of ambivalent about the whole thing."

"How are things with Robert?" Emily asks.

Hannah carefully folds a napkin into a miniature fan. "Oh, fine," she says, concentrating on her creation. "We just don't talk about it anymore."

"Hannah, that's the problem." Emily pulls the napkin through Hannah's fingers. "You've both *got* to be incredibly unhappy. And the kids and Rosa are caught in the middle of it."

"Rosa and I aren't speaking these days."

"You can't deny your feelings, Hannah."

"I can't leave my husband for my yoga instructor."
"C'mon. Rosa's a lot more than your yoga instructor."

*   *   *

"I'm delighted to be at The Club tonight," Lucy says, surveying her eager listeners. "It's a warm place for me in many ways. And it's especially nice to be here this time of year, March being Women's History Month." She begins playing a swaggering melody. "If we were really good, we'd get a whole year." Laughter plays across the audience.

"A couple of years ago, I sat down to write a song about inspirational women. Women who fought not only for civil rights, but for *human* rights. . . . This song is called 'Master's Tools'."

I lean forward as if this will allow me to record the lyrics, which come like a thousand poignant aphorisms.

*

Soujourner Truth questions
Don't she deserve the best place?
She cries out
Voices of bondage, labor, and grief
Ain't she a woman?

Zora Neale Hurston writes
Remembers all she can't forget
She speaks up
Inscribes loves and lives of women
Their dream is the truth

Angela Davis raises her fist
Spits in the face of racism
She fights back
Turn hatred into victories
Create new community

Audre Lorde calls to us
Make differences into strengths
She demands change
The master's tools never dismantle
The master's house

Women, raise your voices
None are free until all are free
Speak the dream
Put down the master's tools
Abandon the master's house
Build a new place to live
Build a new place to live

＊

Brian moves silently up the left aisle and sits a few rows in front of me. His curly hair shifts and bends toward his neighbor. The shiny silver earrings that swing in response must belong to Sharon. They share a muted conversation, then turn their attention to Lucy. Both nod slightly, rhythmically, to her song.

＊   ＊   ＊

"This tour has been especially difficult for me," Lucy says, between songs. The audience relaxes, many leaning back in their seats, indulging her storytelling.

"Last fall I was playing Midwest college towns. It was one of the few times I've felt politically powerless. It seemed like the students who were working on racism hadn't met the people working on class issues, who hadn't met the feminists. . . . And I was there holding the torch, but it was getting wobbly. So I wrote this next song, 'Music Heals.' I'd like to sing it for you." Lucy bows her head as she plays, buttery hair falling into her eyes.

＊

Open eyes and closed minds
Blank stares bruise and wound

Music speaks to our hearts
Music heals through our skin

＊

A hum of appreciation radiates from the audience as Lucy finishes the song and quiets the guitar with the flat of her hand. "Thanks. I'll be back after a short break."

＊   ＊   ＊

I survey the concession table, touching the artifacts for sale. Clumsy stacks of CDs, an order form with Lucy's face and crowded with praise for her music, T-shirts emblazoned with a cacophony of typefaces. I can't make out the message tucked into the folds of the T-shirts, but I see a woman purchase one of the heathery garments and follow her into the women's restroom, hoping to decipher the message.

When I enter, she's holding the T-shirt in front of her, looking at herself in the mirror. Her reflected eyes meet mine. She smiles.

"Think it'll fit?" she asks.

"Sure. What's it say?"

She turns to face me. Her eyes are a watery blue. Turquoise sunbursts dangle from her earlobes. I look down at the T-shirt, stretched across her. Its azure and silver colors mirror her own. She reads the message aloud.

DON'T YOU *SEE* HOW *LOVELY* **YOU** ARE
DON'T **YOU** *KNOW* HOW **MUCH**
YOU HAVE TO **GIVE**
DON'T YOU FEEL **IT'S** TIME TO START
DON'T LET ANYONE **TELL** *YOU*
HOW TO **LIVE**

As she speaks, another woman enters the cramped room. They smile in greeting, and both begin to sing the message, their melody filling the small space.

"That's beautiful," I say.

"I *love* it," the azure woman says, hugging the T-shirt to her. "Hold this?" She thrusts the garment toward me, then tugs at her own black T-shirt, deftly pulling it over her shiny hair. She plies the new raiment from my fingers and turns toward the mirror. Her back folds in soft pillows around the press of her brassiere, then disappears beneath the T-shirt, the mantra.

She turns to face us and pulls at the object of her affection.

"What do you think?" she asks. Without answer she announces, "It's me."

*   *   *

"Hey," Sharon calls when she sees me approaching the ticket desk. "How's your project coming? You almost through?"

"I should be," I say, then reconsider. "I'm getting close. Do you have a minute?"

"Sure."

"It's been a while since we talked. . . . Have things improved with Brian and Ricky?"

"Actually, no. Ricky resigned last week."

"*Really?* How come?"

"He's been pretty unhappy the past few months. I think it had to do with the board's recommendation that he work more closely with Brian in making the booking decisions. I guess Brian's lobbying in that respect paid off."

"How so?"

"The board asked Brian to oversee the bookings. Anything over five thousand dollars had to be approved by both Brian and the board."

"Which made Ricky angry?" I suggest.

"Right. He felt like he'd been demoted. And he just kept boiling over in board meetings and with the staff. He's threatened to quit before, you know."

"Will this stick?"

"The board's taking him seriously. They've offered me the position temporarily."

"Yeah?"

"Well, I guess I offered myself. I'll be working under Brian's direction, though. Not as co-manager."

"I'm sure Brian's happy about that."

"Everybody's pretty excited."

"I hope it works out for you. Congratulations."

"Thanks. We'll see how it goes."

"Interesting news. How about Virginia?"

"I'm afraid that's not a very happy ending either," Sharon sighs.

"Why?"

"After almost a year of trying, she just got tired of a community that wouldn't work to encourage diversity. She didn't see how this organization *could* change or even *wanted* to change, so she left us. I'm really sorry about that."

"Do *you* think the organization wants to change?"

"We've *got* to change. Funding is scarce. Our community is a closed one. We don't operate efficiently and we're outgrowing our facility. People don't want to face the inevitable."

"What do you think will happen?"

"Ricky's leaving forces us to change. We're pretty set in our ways for a so-called 'alternative' music community, but we'll find a way to update ourselves without losing sight of our values. Or the music."

"Values?"

"Our value of space. And musical excellence. The two go hand-in-hand."

"Space?"

"Space for voices that wouldn't be heard in this community if it weren't for our stage. Tonight's a good example. Lucy's a songwriter from Oregon who runs a very small operation. A *woman* songwriter who runs a very small operation. If it weren't for places like The Club, she couldn't put together a tour. That would be a shame."

"She's a powerful presence."

"Her following is incredible. This is the third time she's played here, and the show sold out. When I hear everyone singing along, I know that all the mistakes we make and the disagreements we have are worth it. They *have* to be, because we're smart enough to book someone like Lucy."

"With you doing the bookings, this place is bound to get smarter."

Sharon smiles. "I'm optimistic."

"I am too. Thanks, Sharon. I know you're busy. Just wanted to check in."

"Anytime," Sharon says, then disappears into the crowd.

I go outside to get some air. I think about all the changes The Club has experienced—the rotating cast of employees, board members, performers, and audience members who've devoted their time to The Club over the last thirty years. People with diverse talents, interests, agendas. How do they keep this place going? What binds them together?

The word "persistence" flashes in my mind. It's how Cynthia Lont describes the ability of a "subcultural" organization to survive in an ever-changing mainstream culture without losing its identity.[3] Persistence is the struggle to balance seemingly incompatible goals: profit and the accomplishment of political agendas. She rejects other concepts that might explain this struggle—adaption, co-optation, appropriation, commercialization, commodification[4]—in favor of *persistence*. I understand persistence to be:

> Political tenacity in the face of economic need.
>
> A web of tensions as the organization struggles inside its own structure, in the culture outside it, and in the fuzzy spaces in between.
>
> Myriad catalysts within/between cultures . . . social, economic, political constraints and freedoms; artists and audiences; acts and artifacts.
>
> The interminable push, pull, press of tension/change/resolution . . . tension/change/resolution . . . tension/change/resolution. . . .

" 'Persistence' describes The Club," I say to myself, though I'd argue the struggle lies not between politics and profit, but rather between musical ideals (which, of course, involve politics) and economic viability (which, of necessity, involves not profit, but success as a nonprofit enterprise).

"Persistence also makes sense in light of the multiple cultural competenc*ies* and capit*als* I've discovered—the complex negotiations between musical and social texts that validate the social experience of subcultural actors.[5] The *performances* in which these knowledges are created and shared, contested and reified, are *acts* of persistence . . . however momentary, they are acts of organizational and cultural affirmation and change." I smile, feeling satisfied with my analysis.

I decide to go inside, but pause to stare at a Volkswagen van parked right in front of The Club. A bumper sticker affixed to the back window catches my eye.

"What about women's music?" I ask aloud. "How does it figure in this organization's persistence? Or *does* it?"

*   *   *

"I hope my first set satisfied your political urges . . . and the intermission satisfied your capitalistic urges," Lucy says, leaning into the microphone, as she settles into her guitar and perches on the edge of her stool.

"I had a very nice request during the break. A woman said, 'Please, please, play "Home." I need to hear it.' How can I refuse a request like that?"

Lucy brushes the strings of her guitar. She sings, her voice beams of sunlight.

*

When the world is pulling you
In every direction
And life weighs on you
Holds you down as a stone
Follow where your heart leads
Find your way home

Mother, I see the pain in your smile
In birth and in losing
You found gifts in all
Stripped sorrow to bone
Now, follow where your heart leads
Find your way home

Sister, I see the future in your eyes
Shining, a bright star
So many longings, so many ties
Will you meet morning alone?
Yes, follow where your heart leads
Find your way home

When the world is pulling you
In every direction
And life weighs on you
Holds you down as a stone
Follow where your heart leads
Find your way home

It is in the journey that
You find your way home

*

"Robert?"

"Hannah. Hi."

"How're the kids?" Hannah hunches over the phone and twists the cord around her finger. Lucy's voice seeps through the thin walls that separate the lobby from the main room.

"They're fine. In bed. Zoe finally pulled that front tooth today."

"I threatened to pull it myself if it was still hanging there when I got home."

"When *are* you coming home?"

Hannah is silent, not sure how to answer. She pulls at the neck of her new T-shirt, suddenly rough against her skin.

"Rosa called today. She wants to know," Robert says, his voice cracking.

"I'm not sure." Trembling fingers find solace in the message she wears over her heart. "Robert, I don't think I can come home. Not like before."

"I know, Hannah. But we need you here."

*   *   *

"I'll do the song I always close with," Lucy says. A cheer erupts from the audience.

"But before I play it for you, I'd like us all to give a big thank-you to The Club. In an era when there's almost no money for the arts, the people of The Club walk on water." The audience responds with another burst of passionate applause.

Lucy smiles and plays the opening bars of the song, then stops. "I'd like to dedicate this to anyone who's feeling a little less than beautiful tonight. . . ."

*

Don't you see how lovely you are
Don't you know how much you have to give
Don't you feel it's time to start
Don't let anyone tell you how to live

*

The audience's harmony echoes Lucy's words. *I* echo her words. The song has only this one verse, and we sing it over and over, momentum building around us, our voices a tide of emotion. Tears sting my eyes. I look to every corner of the room and see mouths and bodies moving to our communal rhythm.

The song slowly fades and a thunder of applause fills the space. I sit frozen in my chair, unable to describe what I've just witnessed. The audience provides a barrage of half-sentences as they brush past me . . .

"spiritual"	"invigorating"	"so *happy*"	"just for me"
"energizing"	*"200 close friends"*	*"wow"*	*"I don't know how"*

. . . eager to get into the night, their cars, their favorite coffee shops, itching to talk about the performance.

I record their thoughts as they march by, then stand to make my own way home. I see Brian talking to a woman—young, crocheted beret slipping slightly over one eye, tiny steno pad in her hands. As I pass I hear him say, "The Club is a sort of shrine of a kind to a particular kind of music. We're a way of life."

Fieldnotes . . . .

3.24.96
The Club, 7:30–10:30 p.m.

My enthusiasm for this project—even for writing fieldnotes—has been renewed! Last night I saw Lucy Rodney perform. It was a magical evening of music, and community . . . and insight. It was as if everything fell into place. The lines between audience and performer were blurred as the music moved from the stage through the room. People sang along, providing harmony for Lucy's songs of inspiration and struggle. True to her women's music sisters, Lucy sang to women—lovers, friends, and mothers—and to men, children, and animals, sending a message of strength, respect, tenderness.[6]

And in the idea of persistence, I believe I've found a way to understand how The Club negotiates myriad inter- and extra-organizational interests and tensions, as well as the pressures and capitulations of subcultural and mainstream cultural influences.

Persistence describes the multiplicitous struggles and successes of an organization striving to balance musical ideals against economic viability.

Persistence is the push-and-pull of Brian and Ricky's struggle for influence over the bookings, Virginia's insistence that The Club's audiences and artists be more diverse, Sharon's worry about a community—her community—that seems so slow to change, Mitchell's concern for the integrity of the music.

Persistence is the incessant give-and-take, selfishness and sacrifice of Lina's life on the road. It's Elaine's struggle to perform her identity as an artist and a lesbian. It's Cheryl's desire to carry her community with her. Persistence is Patty's tireless devotion to leftist political goals. It's Chris' and Kathy's dedication to traditional country music. It's Lucy's unwavering sense of direction—musically, culturally, socially, and politically.

Persistence is the perpetual intermingling of irony and earnest good intention in using cultural categorization to measure out arts monies, in celebrating Black History Month or Women's History Month, in deciding on an artist's or organization's role in these ephemeral tributes.

These tensions, sacrifices, and ironies surface, if only for a moment, in the performances staged at The Club. In bursts and glimpses, persistence is *performed* in the music presented there. In moments of mystery and communion, we experience cultural knowledges and practices—of organizational, community, subcultural, and cultural actors—voiced, silenced, fragmented, and refracted.

Women's music performances may provide a *particular* and *fleeting* vision of this persistence. Traditionally, women's music has provided artists and audiences with a means of redefining self, creating opportunities for new identities and social potentials, and portraying an alternative set of values (Lont, "Between Rock and a Hard Place" 95).

Performance provides a *medium* through which participants embody these selves, identities, potentials, and values, using music to illustrate and interrogate the existing social order (Robertson 225). Women's music can thus function as an act of organizational, community, and subcultural persistence for performers and audiences . . . although persistence may not be experienced by all present at the site of the performance–those who do not consider themselves part of women's music subculture or the organization's subculture.

It's also important to note that these performances are created within and through women's bodies, which requires me to ask questions about the social construction of gender identities, and, further, how these social constructions are *performed* in music. Here persistence takes on a new meaning. It's no longer a term that describes only the *activities* of members of organizations or subcultures, but also the *social experience of gender*, as well as the performative resistance and reification of a naturalized maleness and heterosexuality. Persistence, in this sense, embodies a performance aesthetics that "marks the contested and fluctuating rates of exchange among sexuality, performance, and power" (Fiske 104).

Viewing women's music performances at The Club in terms of persistence, as I've described it here, illustrates the postmodern condition of performance. These performances are fragmented, plural, layered, and constantly changing enactments of culture. They're snapshots of participants' realities. And yet, in the heat and flesh of performance, these pictures become quite indistinguishable from the images they depict (Connor 61). Text and performance, participant and artist, intersect and collide in a dizzying array of meanings and realities.

This intermingling of social reality and cultural performance is not accomplished without the myriad tensions–resistance and accommodation–characteristic of persistence. Dwight Conquergood articulates the persistent, postmodern character of performance, as well as the critical role ethnographers play in interrogating and explicating these performances:

> Because it is public, performance is a site of struggle where competing interests intersect, and different viewpoints get

articulated. Ethnographers are now asking, How does performance reproduce, legitimate, uphold, or challenge, critique, and
subvert ideology . . . ? How are performances situated between
forces of accommodation and resistance? And how do they
simultaneously reproduce and struggle against hegemony?
("Poetics, Play, Process, and Power" 84)

Conquergood's questions are those of *performative* persistence, and as an ethnographer, I . . .

"Interrogating and explicating? Resistance and accommodation? Persistence? *Boooring!*" The words appear on my computer
screen, but I'm not writing them.

"Excuse me?" I type.

"What happened to your postmodern narrative?"

"It's still here," I type in half-hearted defense. "Who are you?"

"It's me, Nick."

"I'm working on theory here. . . ." I begin.

"And you should. Just don't lose sight of the story." The words
burn into the monitor.

"Here, read this sentence: '. . . *writing* sociology is the unexam-
ined way in which we mask and inscribe our desire to shape
history.'"[7]

"Laurel?" I type.

"I'm here too," she writes. "How might you use theory to
examine your own writing?"

"Nick, here. Laurel's got a good point. How can you be more
reflexive in your writing—about theory, your fieldwork, your narrative?"

"Yes. Position yourself as knower and teller?"[8] This from
Laurel.

"How about story . . . a performative story?" I offer.

"I'm glad to be here tonight," I murmur into the microphone, then offer a nervous laugh. I'm not used to hearing my voice projected in a room.

"As most of you know, I've been working on a research project at The Club for the past two years . . . I've had wonderful talks and experiences here with employees and board members, artists and audiences, especially at women's music performances. And as I struggled with ways to write about these experiences, and with ways to give something back to this truly inspirational organization, I came up with the idea for tonight's show."

I bring the guitar to my chest. Bruised fingertips find their pained places on the strings. "Tonight, we'll sing songs of The Club—its people and its music. But before we begin, I'd like to introduce my friends on stage . . . Lina Michaels, Elaine Baker, Cheryl Wheeler, Patty Sanders, Kathy Campbell and Chrissy Lovell, and Lucy Rodney. These women are my inspiration. Their generosity made tonight possible." The crowd—mostly white and mostly women—responds with a loud and enthusiastic welcome.

As they applaud, I take a moment to survey the house. Don offers a smile of encouragement from the front row. He sits next to the bearded man and his wife.

The regulars who've accompanied me to every performance—the leathered man and the gangly couple—sit in the third row, off to my right.

Mitchell, Sharon, and Virginia share a table near the concession counter.

Colleen and Jerry work the sound.

Nick, Gerri, and Bill relax in the back, a tiny candle illuminating stacks of paper on their table—paper filled with my stories.

Ricky and Brian are silhouetted in the doorway to the outer lobby.

"We're all here," I think. The quiet attention of the audience tears me from my thoughts.

"We'd like to begin with a number that pays tribute to The Club and its vital presence in the community," I say, feeling a pang of nervousness. It's called 'Persistence'."

*

In the window of a used furniture store
She sees the faint outlines of a dream
Scorns her critics, unlocks the heavy door
Untangles cobwebs, brews cups of belief

Music dances in flickering candlelight
Nurtures a community frail and tender
Listeners intent, musicians find flight
In the freedom of a mother's tether

Some nights it's hard to open the door
But people still come, stand in the rain
Serve fragrant joe or sweep the floor
They stave off failure's night 'til day

Make music's hearth a safe place
For songs of love and resistance
Play in culture's bittersweet band
Join string and voice with heart and hand
In fearless acts of persistence

Mother weeps weary farewell tears
Music's children are uncertain, afraid
To roll up melodies, pack their fears
And seek new shelter for a fragile stage

Forsaken warehouse bids hushed invitation
Cinder block lovingly embraces the alone
Lodges cast-off chairs, tattered dedication
Builds music's strong and gentle home

Newfound tests have a familiar melody
How many women, Blacks, Asians, others,
How many gays, lesbians do you employ?
Money dances, fettered to their answers

Make music's hearth a safe place
For songs of love and resistance
Play in culture's bittersweet band
Join string and voice with heart and hand
In defiant acts of persistence

The politics of profit and loss
Don't mean anything
If music's not skill and truth
Don't mean anything
Without a place to hear
Without a place to play our lives

Make music's hearth a safe place
For songs of love and resistance
Play in culture's bittersweet band
Join string and voice with heart and hand
In selfless acts of persistence
Selfless acts of persistence

*

The waves of applause startle me. I look over at Lucy, unsure what to do next. She offers a radiant smile, then pulls the microphone close to her lips.

"Thank you," she says for me. The glaring stage lights blur my vision, make the crowd seem a sea of glowing candles and bright eyes, buoyed by earnest appreciation.

And yet there's something frantic in the desire that radiates from them . . . wanting the sound, the lyrics. Willing us to please them so they might praise us, an endless coupling. I feel suddenly hot.

"We'd like to do a number called 'My Song a Window'," Lucy says, rescuing me from my confusion. "It brings together our feelings about women's music and women performers."

"But we wrote it in the third person," Lina adds, "because we knew it could apply not just to us, but to many, many people."

*

Eyes hard on her face, her body, her fingertips
Seeing right past her, recognizing someone else
Seeing right through her, gazing at her soul
Her song a mirror, the music takes its toll

Some nights she feels like a puppet singer
Pulled and pushed by wanton strings
Playing their melodies and baring her legs
Hungry front-row eyes don't need to beg

Her lover's touch an open question
Her lyrics, each note a firm suggestion
Of a life they paint on a gendered canvas
Blind hate or love, their strokes guiltless

They twist her words, claim knower's rights
To meanings and messages she didn't write
Feed culture's fire with playwright's fantasy
Of men and women, hatred and ecstasy

Eyes hard on her face, her body, her fingertips
Seeing right past her, recognizing someone else
Seeing right through her, gazing at her soul
Her song a mirror, the music takes its toll

Other dusks bring voices loving and calm
Their chorusing passion a soothing balm
Singing together stories no longer her own
Women and men, friends, lovers, alone

Not harsh questions but gentle replies
Mouths aching to birth plaintive cries
Songs teaching lessons of patience
Gender troubled in sweet persistence

This play of deep collaboration and trust
Her fingers weave acts of love, lust
Their harmony a heartbeat of consent
For performances that resist, relent

Eyes light on her face, her body, her fingertips
Seeing only her, knowing well her secrets
Seeing inside her, understanding all
Her song a window, the music feeds her soul

Eyes light on my face, my body, my fingertips
Seeing only me, knowing well my secrets
Seeing inside of me, understanding all
My song a window, the music feeds my soul

✴

The sound of our collective voices—silvery and spare, angry and rau-cous—fades as it floats over the crowd. Tears of sweat cool my face, ease my breathing. I look out over them, their eyes hungry and soft.

"We'd like to do one more before we take a break," I say. "This next song has great personal significance . . . I hope you'll indulge me. It's called 'How Do I'?" I breathe deeply and feel my fingers move, unguided, over the strings.

✴

How do I describe it
This place, this song, this night
When everything is jaded
Colored by my mind

How do I uncover it
The place where music hides
Each note syncopated
In songs of disguise

How do I read it
Look into plaintive eyes
Understand woman's aching
Her life a compromise

How do I interpret it
Audience's unfailing gaze
As surveillance or as longing
To possess the artist's muse

How do I criticize it
Paint portraits of inequity
In acceptance and belonging
Confused hatred, bigotry

How do I explain it
Intricate weave of lives
When all your words have faded
Blurred into prose and lies

How do I rewrite it
Let your voices shine
Crystallize and seclude it
Your world from mine

How do I escape it
This place you call a home
Leave your music behind
Find a song of my own

*

The last note hangs in the air, the audience silent. "Thanks," I say, my voice cracking. "We'll be back after a short intermission." The lights have set my skin on fire once again. In the flurry of applause, I prop my guitar in the stand and hurry down the stage steps.

I look for Sharon or Virginia or Mitchell in the surge of smiles and eyes that moves toward me, but I don't see them.

Brian and Ricky have abandoned their watch at the door.

Don waits patiently for me outside in the night air.

I stop, searching for Nick and Gerri and Bill, but see only the flickering candle on their table, its Formica top covered with my stories. As I stand over the paper-strewn table, the music echoes in my ears. Glowing candle wax descends in rhythmic droplets, blurring my uncertain words from the pages.

Notes

1. Zora Neale Hurston, *Their Eyes Were Watching God*, 1937, foreword by Mary Helen Washington, afterword by Henry Louis Gates, Jr. (San Bernardino, Calif.: Borgo, 1990), 1.
2. Edith Evans, quoted in *The Harper Book of Quotations*, ed. Robert I. Fitzhenry, 3rd ed. (New York: HarperCollins, 1993), 411.
3. Cynthia Lont, "Persistence of Subcultural Organizations: An Analysis Surrounding the Process of Organizational Change," *Communication Quarterly* 38.1 (1990): 3. The author defines subcultures as localized and differentiated social structures within larger, dominant cultures. Subcultures are characterized by their resistance to, and interaction with, the larger culture to which they belong.
4. Lont, 9–10. The author rejects these terms because they characterize organizational change *either* as change that comes from within the organization (adaptation, commercialization) or as change affected by forces outside the organization (co-optation, appropriation, commodification)—as opposed to the notion of mutual tensions (inside the organization and out) and mutual sites of change and resistance to change. These perspectives are further limited by their discrete, rather than processual, focus as well as by a failure to consider cultural forces in favor of solely economic relationships.
5. John Fiske, *Television Culture* (London: Routledge, 1987), 19. The author explains that cultural competence "involves a critical understanding of the text and the conventions by which it is constructed, it involves the bringing of both textual and social experience to bear upon the [music, the performance] at the moment of reading. . . . Cultural capital and cultural competence are both central to people's ability to make socially pertinent and pleasurable meanings from the semiotic resources of the text."
6. Lont, "Between Rock and a Hard Place: A Model of Subcultural Persistence and Women's Music," diss., University of Iowa, 1984, 93. These "messages" are noted by Lont in her analysis of the character and content of women's music.
7. Laurel Richardson, "Postmodern Social Theory: Representational Practices," *Sociological Theory* 9.2 (1991): 174.
8. Richardson, "Writing: A Method of Inquiry," *Handbook of Qualitative Research*, ed. Norman K. Denzin and Yvonna S. Lincoln (Thousand Oaks, Calif.: Sage, 1994), 520. The author asserts that experimental writers "raise and display postmodernist issues," including the question of "how the author positions the Self as knower and teller." Thus, experimental writers must ask questions about self and other, as well as about authorial objectivity, reflexivity, and representation.

We have no models for scientific knowledge that account for nonhierarchic learning, and we may have to borrow from the poet, the artist, the madman, the mystic.

Yvonna Lincoln, "The Making of a Constructivist"[1]

I am thinking of the onion again . . . Not self-righteous like the proletarian potato, nor a siren like the apple. No show-off like the banana. But a modest, self-effacing vegetable, questioning, introspective, peeling itself away, or merely radiating halos like lake ripples.

Erica Jong, "Fruits and Vegetables"[2]

I know what you're going through. Writing a thesis feels impossible. When it's all over, you just want to collapse.

Sharon, night manager of The Club

As long as she writes little notes nobody objects to a woman writing.

Virginia Woolf, *Orlando*[3]

7

Little Notes

"WHAT DO YOU think you'll write about?" Natalie asks as she thrusts a steaming cup of coffee in my direction. Our interview is long over, but we've lingered on her sunny porch, talking.

"Well, it's hard to say right now," I begin, sipping my coffee. Too hot. "I want to write about The Club's culture and communication and how these things are realized and experienced through music. I want to write about how The Club negotiates various interests and challenges—musical, organizational, social, and political—and still manages to stay afloat. I want to write about women's music performances and about women performers. I want to write about my experience as an ethnographer. I want to write something that captures the mystery and magic of this organization. I *don't* want to write some detached, scientific account. . . . I'm rambling, aren't I?"

She looks at me for a long moment. "Just tell the story."

*   *   *

"I don't know why we couldn't do this in the morning," I say to no one. I've been pacing around the house all day. *The* day. My thesis defense. It feels more like a defense of my life as a scholar. My writing. The Club. Women's music. All of it. The phone rings with reassuring regularity, but I let everyone, even Don, speak words of encouragement to the empty purr of the answering machine. No word from Gerri, Bill, or Nick. I check my e-mail one last time before leaving for the conference room, before facing the barrage of questions. There's a message from Nick.

Subj:	Good luck
Date:	20 May 1996
From:	nickt@csus.edu
To:	stacyhj@aol.com

Good luck this afternoon. I think you're ready, but this will be a defense, not a party. That means you'll have to defend your choices. Why The Club? (Why not the Dead?) Why ethnography? Why this form of writing? How is it reliable/valid? How is your story postmodern/feminist? How has your thesis fallen short of your goals? How did being a woman influence the work? What are the implications of this work? You'll do fine, but again, it is supposed to be a defense. Later, Nick

"Later is now," I say. I pile my thesis, my fieldnotes, my typed and categorized defenses in the back seat of the car. I push a homemade cassette into the tape deck and grip the steering wheel tight. Cheryl Wheeler's voice wraps around me. I play her song, her rhythm and poetry, over and over, singing loud to drown out shrill voices of doubt.

*　　*　　*

I am waiting.

My fingers have gone cold and thin, blood pounds in my ears. I stare at my colleagues—teachers, friends, scholars, women—across the conference room table, its faux wood a sea of separation. Bronzed lips smile, but my eyes return an empty stare. Motherly, sisterly concern wraps silently around me and I push it off.

Footsteps and laughter. Here they come. Bill first, his wavy hair and deliberate gait somehow entering the room before him, wistful grin trailing behind. Then Gerri, smiling and warm in white. She looks at me, wills me confidence. And Nick, his baseball cap and shorts camouflaging serious questions.

My final performance. A play in justification and explanation—of *my* words about *other* people, presented to still *other* people. A parody in which I defend my choices, including the choice to include myself. A simulacra[4] of the ethnography, the performances, the writing, the ethnographer and the participants. Conjuring them all up in a sterile room before the tribunal of hyperreality.

*　　*　　*

"I'd like to begin by welcoming everyone," Gerri says. The onlookers rustle in their seats, then settle in for the ride. I sit rigid, trying to remember my lines.

"We'll begin with a few questions about the thesis. Nick, why don't we start with you?"

"Sure," he says, offering a half-moon grin. I look at him and have no idea what he's thinking or what he will say. Nick knows more about me than almost anyone here . . . but we're connected by our writing. Now, sitting across from me, he's a stranger. I want to suggest we do this over e-mail.

"You say you've written a postmodern ethnography. I'd like to talk about the theoretical implications of this choice, but first, let's start with methodology."

I furiously scan the pages in front of me. Of course I'd written it down, an elaborate discussion of my methodological choices. But my voice is gone. I look at Nick.

The door opens and two leathery old men shuffle into the room. I know them. I've seen them at conferences, circled by an ever-present congregation of graduate students. They're the Methodology brothers—Reliability and Validity. They both have brilliantly white hair and a penchant for perpetuating the interminable quantitative–qualitative debate. They take seats on either side of Nick and fix an immovable gaze on me.

"Ah, I'm glad you made it," Nick says to them, but looks at me. "Stacy, why don't you spend some time talking with Validity and Reliability about your methodological choices?" His bearded chin jerks, beckoning me to begin. My stomach doubles back on itself.

"Well, as you know," I say, then stop. "Do you know about my work?"

"Yes," Reliability says. "The committee has kept us apprised of your progress. Please continue."

"All right. I'll begin by telling you about my fieldwork. Over the last two years, I've spent approximately seventy-five hours at The Club. This breaks down to forty hours of performances . . . twenty-five hours of interviews with board members, staff, and musicians . . . and ten hours of meetings, document review, working the ticket window. All of this is detailed. . . ."

"How did you select the performances?" Validity interrupts.

"At first I went to a variety of shows—bluegrass, country, world music. I focused on the different audiences The Club drew."

"At first?"

"Yes. Originally, I was interested in how different types of music might serve the interests of various groups within the organization—all of which exist in opposition to mainstream music interests."

Reliability leans forward, frowns. "Did this change?"

"I became interested in women's music, a specific type of music presented at The Club, and decided to refocus my study on those performances."

"You changed the focus of the research?"

"Yes." My cheeks flush with fire.

Validity smiles. "Go on," he urges.

"So I concentrated on women's music performances. . . ."

Reliability inhales loudly, interrupting me. "You interviewed only women's music performers and audiences?"

"No. I started the interviews before I decided to concentrate on women's music. I asked questions about the culture, the role of music in their communication, stories about The Club. As the interviews progressed, I asked people to define women's music. . . ."

"Making your research totally unreliable!" Reliability shouts and pounds his fist on the table.

"How?" I ask defensively.

"Don't you know about measurement reliability?"

"Making sure my measurement is consistent over time, which makes my results reliable over time, which. . . ."

"Changing," he interjects.

"Which has *nothing* to do. . . ."

His voice booms over mine. "Changing the research population—and the interview protocol—*guarantees* that your project is not reliable! The measurement error here is incredible."

Tears sting my eyes. I look around the room, eager to find a friendly face . . . or a way to escape.

"Tell us what you were trying to accomplish in these interviews," Nick says, ignoring Reliability's withering scowl.

"A number of things." I pause to collect my thoughts. I don't want to make any mistakes. "First, I asked questions that gave insight into how people perceived their day-to-day experiences. Altheide and Johnson say ethnographers must be committed to capturing members' experience of their *own* social reality."[5] I look at the brothers, at their empty eyes.

Validity glances over at Reliability, who shakes his head but remains silent.

I exhale, realize I'm holding my breath. "And I began some very rewarding relationships during these interviews."

"Relationships with your subjects?" Reliability demands, raising his voice.

A wave of dread sweeps over me. "More like collaborators."

Validity's eyes widen. "Young lady, we have a big problem with objectivity here!"

Anger rises in my throat. "Maybe, if you view objectivity as a way to *objectify* those you study!"

Gerri leans into the conversation. "I think Stacy's attention to multiple perspectives illustrates her recognition of the pluralistic nature of qualitative research."[6]

"It was more than that," I say. "This was more than just *my* thesis. I looked at it as a collaborative work. . . . The members' voices had to be present."

Reliability laughs, then chokes on his own amusement. "It's not a thesis at all," he croaks.

I cannot speak.

"A thesis," Validity begins, waving the *Guide to Graduate Studies* above his head, "is a 'written, systematic study of a research problem'."[7]

Reliability nods. "It must identify a research question, articulate the importance of the study, describe the methods for gathering information, analyze the data collected, and state the significance of the findings."

"You must use rigorous methodological and analytical procedures, *and* you must make a *contribution* to theory," Validity says.

"Isn't that what I've done?"

"No!" Reliability spits. "What you've done is string together a few awkward lines of prose. This is a collection of immature musings, *little notes*. It is not scholarship."

The fire returns to my cheeks. I think of all my field notebooks, my stories . . . pages and pages of "little notes." " 'As long as she writes little notes nobody objects to a woman writing',"[8] I whisper.

"Did you say something, young lady?" he asks.

"No."

"Maybe we need to talk about the criteria we developed to assess Stacy's work. I think you'll find this discussion illuminating," Nick says. "Stacy?"

I take a deep breath. "Well, the criteria really grew out of my commitment to a feminist and postmodern project." I look to Reliability for some sign to continue. He stares back at me, eyes frozen pools. "Once I decided to focus on women's music, feminist and postmodern thought showed me how to shape the methodology."

Validity's voice breaks our stare. "You'll need to explain."

"I can." I riffle through my notes. "OK, here it is. Feminism also focuses on cultural practices—the ways gender differences are created and reified, normalized. The idea is to articulate power discrepancies and work for the elimination of these arbitrary gender differences."[9]

Reliability and Validity look bored. My heart races.

I feel them slipping away.

"And," I say, my words coming faster, "feminism works to reclaim knowledge for women and empower them to speak by being reflexive, being multivocal, and making room for personal experience."

Reliability glares at me. "You failed to address postmodernism."

"I was getting to that. Postmodernism and feminism are compatible because postmodern culture is seen as densely *contextual*—a complex network of power relationships that are constantly shifting and changing. These relationships are most 'visible' to us in discourse. . . . Discourse reveals, and I'm quoting Patti Lather here, the 'interactive complexity, shifting-centered, and multi-sited constructedness of our selves and our worlds'."[10]

"You are trying my patience, young woman!" Reliability huffs. "What is the connection between postmodernism and feminism?"

"A postmodern feminism questions not only the role of gender, but also race and sexual preference, in oppression based on *difference*. . . . It views difference as *culturally constructed* through discourse, not as something determined by biology."[11]

Reliability's cheeks balloon. He blasts hot air at me. "Doesn't postmodernism deny the legitimacy of 'women' as a category?"

"Feminism has struggled to eliminate discourse that essentializes and categorizes women's experience. Rather than deny it, I think postmodernism highlights the *struggle* of women to live and speak within and outside categories."

"But we're concerned about . . ." Reliability begins.

"Postmodern feminism," I interrupt, "encourages self-reflexivity and critique by questioning its very form, method, import—by questioning the *process* of scholarship."

Reliability shakes his head wearily. "What makes *your* process scholarship and another's journalism or a work of fiction? How are we to judge this work?"

"Tell us why you chose to do an ethnographic study," Bill suggests.

"In order to enact—no, to *perform*—a postmodern, feminist perspective, I needed to experience the culture first-hand . . . I wanted to be involved with the people I was studying and aware of my positioning in this process."

"So ethnographic methods are both the means of conducting research and the criteria for judging it? If that isn't tautological. . . ."

Gerri shoots him an angry look. "Let's hear what she has to say about ethnography."

"For me, ethnography is deeply intermingled with postmodernism, feminism, performance. . . ." I pause to flip through my notes. The clock ticks loudly, each second eroding my confidence.

"Fabian has defined ethnography as 'a search for understanding that begins with cultural performance,' "[12] I say, not recognizing my trembling voice. I wait for Reliability or Validity to begin the inquisition, but they are silent. Reliability's chin lolls on his chest. His eyes are closed.

"Stephen Tyler says postmodern ethnography is 'the mutual, dialogical production of a discourse, a story of sorts.'[13] In other words, postmodern ethnography is dynamic, performative." Reliability's head bobs gently to the rhythm of my words. Validity sighs.

"How is it performative?" Nick asks.

"I think Conquergood says it best. He says ethnography isn't mimesis—imitation—or poesis—construction. Ethnography is *kinesis*—dynamic motion, performative.[14] It is a multiple, sensuous, and fragmented collaboration of authors and texts that intensifies everyday experience."[15]

Reliability's eyes fly open. "If this is a cooperative project, how do you accomplish your feminist objectives? Is feminism a goal of your collaborators?"

"Not all of them," I say, mildly.

"Then how did you reconcile your research agenda with the experience of the members?"

His words bruise me. "I struggled with this question. . . ."

"Weren't you picking up on the feminist ideals of a subculture within the organization?" Nick offers.

"Yes," I say, thankful. "I *did* encounter a feminist subculture in women's music performances. Focusing on these performances seemed natural and right for me. *And* for the members. I didn't impose my agenda on anyone."

Reliability coughs. "You can't grasp what we're telling you. This research is *flawed, solipsistic*."

"It is flawed and selfish," I say, "if you believe in a single, objective reality, the possibility of detached observation, and empirical verification. But a feminist, postmodern ethnography has shown me multiple, culturally constructed realities, the creative interaction among researcher and participant, and the dialectic process of scholarship."[16]

"Have you captured these realities, this process in writing the thesis?" Validity asks. "This seems more like a novel to me. It's hard to tell where cultural knowledge ends and creative writing begins."

"You're right," I say. "What I've written *is* a collection of *little notes*. But does that mean they can't teach us anything about this culture, or women's music performances, or the process of ethnography? The writing is integral to my project. . . ."

"Tell us about that," Gerri says.

I swallow hard, pushing back my tears. "Feminist ethnography bridges the gap 'between feminist commitment and textual innovation.'[17] The postmodern ethnographic text is physical. Spoken. Performed. Tyler says it's a text 'to read not with the eyes alone, but with the ears in order to hear the voices of the pages'."[18]

I meet Validity's stare. "Such a text allows me to work toward the goals of postmodern feminist ethnography . . . to be reflexive, multivocal; to make room for personal experience."

I feel sick, false, trying to defend my choices by talking with a certainty I don't feel, a certainty my feminist goals deny.

"You still haven't addressed the criteria to be used in judging your work," Validity says. "How do your postmodern, feminist, performative ideas and methods allow you to create scholarship that is both a valid and reliable source of knowledge?"

"They don't."

"*What?*" Validity asks.

"Reliability and validity are criteria rooted in the positivist paradigm. As I've explained before . . ."

Reliability glowers at me. "What are you saying?"

"I'm not sure you're the best people to judge my work."

"Your impudence is becoming quite tiring," he says.

"All I'm saying is there are other ways to view reality. Other criteria for assessing the process of scholarship."

"Such as?" Nick asks.

"Egon Guba and Yvonna Lincoln first got me thinking about how our perceptions—our scholarship and knowledge—are *constructed* rather than discovered."

"How so?" Gerri prompts.

"They describe 'states of being' for researchers and participants, rather than methodological 'tests.' The idea is to judge the authenticity of the *process*, rather than the product."[19]

"What are these *states of being?*" Reliability demands.

"An awareness of the researcher's construction of reality, the appreciation of other's constructions, the ability of the inquiry to prompt and then enable social, cultural, and political action for *all* involved,"[20] I say.

"Did your work enable that kind of action?" Nick asks.

"I, I'm not sure. I'd like to think that it has, but. . . ."

"That's all well and good," Validity waves his hand, dismissing my confession. "But we must also be concerned with judging the product of your research. You agree that you have produced a product here."

"Yes," I say, glad that Validity has changed the subject.

"Then how might we judge this product, given your preference for multiple realities and states of being?" Reality asks, contempt punctuating every word.

"I found poststructuralist criteria to be most helpful here," I say, ignoring him. "These criteria focus on multiple, relative realities, the subjective nature of knowledge, and emergent research."[21]

Validity sighs. "You'll need to explain."

"Actually, Patti Lather's concept of 'transgressive validity' works well. She says it provides a way to 'observe the staging of the poses of methodology'."[22]

"*Poses?*" Reliability cries. "How trite."

The door creaks, then swings wide.

"Ah, I'm glad you made it," Nick says. "Come in, come in."

I crane my neck to see who he's invited, to see my new opponent.

A bald head timidly peers around the doorjamb. Sapphire eyes dance around the room.

"Here," Gerri says, beckoning him with a smile. "Sit here, next to me." The slight man edges into the room and fades into the seat next to Gerri.

I glare at Nick, but he looks past me, his eyes fixed on a woman with crimson lips and powdered-sugar skin. Quick footsteps and taut silk make a shrill melody.

"Who are these people?" I wonder. "What's Nick up to?"

A man with spiky hair and flowing robes stiffly bows his head to clear the doorway, then dwarfs the frail woman as he sits next to her.

He's followed by a man—no, woman—no, *man*—with lush, green eyes.

"Let me introduce our guests," Nick says. "This is Ironic Validity." The bashful man nods solemnly.

"Paralogical and Rhizomatic, there, next to Ironic." The frail woman and imposing man smile.

"And of course, Voluptuous Validity."[23] He—or she—looks away, distracted.

Nick smiles at Reliability and Validity. "Gentlemen, I believe you know them."

"We most certainly do not," Reliability says.

"Don't you recognize your transgressive cousins?" he prods.

Validity coughs. "They aren't our cousins. Why, they look nothing like us."

Nick nods at the newly arrived guests. "Why don't you introduce yourselves?"

The fragile woman stands and thrusts her hand toward the bald man. "This is Ironic Validity," her deep voice booms, startling me. "He is, of course, deaf . . . but he is a profound poet, a master of language."

Ironic shakes his head sharply, and his hands speak in ardent protest. Paralogical watches his contortions, nods, then turns to meet our gaze.

"He says he is both *master* and *slave* to language. . . . His mute poetry of simulation captures our inability to articulate reality, urges us to make multiple and contradictory readings of his verse, impels us to break down the imaginary lines between object, author, text, audience."

Validity frowns. "Bunk!"

"And what do you make of *me?*" Paralogical demands.

"I see a very confused young woman," Validity responds.

I remember her now. I saw her speak on campus last year. She's a film maker . . . lesbian, outspoken, provocative, controversial.

"Precisely!" she shouts at him. "Confused, according to your essentializing stereotypes . . . your homogenizing view of reality!" A ruby smile softens angry eyes. "Am I what you wish me to be?"

"Certainly not."

"Because I don't make sense in your logic. I parody your reading of me—and of her."

She points a scarlet-kissed finger at me, but her eyes remain fixed on the chalky man. "I threaten your tidy interpretation of both of us . . . and yet I can set you free."

"Free from *what?*" Reliability bellows.

"From the stranglehold of Truth," Rhizomatic interrupts. He slowly rises from the chair, his mountainous frame filling the room. "To be free, you must listen to me, to my music."

My stomach tightens. "Music?"

"Yes. Music that resists a singular rhythmic pattern and sensibility. Music that is polyrhythmic and incomplete. Music that requires the listener, the *dancer,* to complete the rhythm."[24]

Validity glares at us. "What does this have to do with *me?*"

"My music produces multiple, contradictory, and unsteady rhythms. It resists static interpretation, renders me *incapable* of creating the music alone. It's the same for women's music, and for her, for this work," he says, jerking his head toward me. Dreadlocks wave mockingly at Validity.

Reliability rips a brilliant yellow page from his notebook, folds it, and passes it to Validity, who peeks between the folds. He smiles, then spreads his fingers out over their secret.

"Voluptuous?" Nick says.

"Ah, yes. I am perhaps the most difficult for you to accept, my cousins." A redolent presence fills the room . . . exotic yet familiar, magnetic yet distant. Difficult because I am created in your male, hegemonic image of knowledge, yet I am also feminine and resistant."

"You can't be both!" Validity challenges. "You're a deviant!"

"I am a performer, an artist of knowledge—not banal and objective as you wish, but reflexive, spirited, creative." A wicked smile paints ample lips.

Reliability and Validity shrink in their seats, their rosy complexions ashen.

"Thank you, Voluptuous," Nick says, then looks at me. "Stacy, can you tell Reliability and Validity how their cousins have influenced your work?"

"I tried to crystallize each of them in my writing."

Reliability smirks. "Crystallize?"

"To reveal the Ironic, Paralogical, Rhizomatic, and Voluptuous possibilities for understanding—and questioning—the multiple 'truths' of this culture."[25]

"I've had enough of this nonsense," Validity says. "Back to *our* question. How is the product—what you've written—a valid and reliable source of knowledge?"

"You're asking me to legitimate *your* vision of knowledge. I can't."

"But you must answer us."

"Why? I understand your vision of reality and the process of inquiry, but I believe in another approach. Is that wrong?"

"No," Validity says. "Unless you want to call yourself a social scientist."

"But for me a social scientist is a curious student of, and creative participant in, everyday life."

"Do you think this declaration relieves you of all responsibility to academic rigor?" Validity bellows.

"I'm not saying my work shouldn't be evaluated. But I didn't test hypotheses created well in advance of my research . . . didn't conduct experiments under carefully controlled conditions. I tried to do something very different."[26]

"What *did* you do?" Nick asks, coming to my rescue.

"I created spaces for multiple knowledges—understandings—of The Club, of women's music performances there. I consulted the poet, the controversial film maker, the musician, and the performance artist,[27] rather than the social scientist, in order to understand this knowledge."

"Were you successful?" Gerri asks.

"I think so."

"What did you accomplish?" Bill inquires.

"I revealed the poetic ineptitude of language, as Ironic does. I followed Paralogical's advice and created a text that challenges these knowledges for the reader. I listened to Rhizomatic's music and wrote my own song, but its rhythm is incomplete without the voices of others. And I followed my heart, as Voluptuous teaches, and challenged patriarchal constructions of culture. I let feminist voices speak. Loudly."

"Did you do this well?" Nick asks.

I look at Nick, Gerri, and Bill. At the brothers. "Yes. I did all of these things well, and yet, I failed."

"Oh?" Reliability says.

"Yes."

"How?" Nick asks.

"I gave into my interpretations, privileged my rhythm over others. I masked the voices of some—musicians, audience members, and employees—in favor of the voices of others. And I failed to write the *silences* of people of color—performers, audience members, women. I succeeded *and* failed in creating a valid text in poststructuralist terms, and if I had it to do again, I might do it very differently. I might not write a text at all."

"That's just it," Rhizomatic says. "The text is always incomplete. If you understand that, you've learned a valuable lesson."

"Ridiculous!" Validity yells, standing.

"Sit *down!*" Paralogical shouts. Her words make him shudder.

"I will not take orders from an insolent *girl!*" he shouts, seething. "Reliability, I suggest we take our leave."

Reliability pushes back from the table and jerks from his chair. He and Validity walk in silent harmony to the door. It slams heavy behind them, sealing the rest of us inside.

I look down at the folded paper of brilliant yellow left behind on the table in front of me. A single word, Reliability's script, stares up at me: *Nihilist*

"Let's take a short break," Gerri suggests. "Ironic, Paralogical, Rhizomatic, Voluptuous, thanks very much for coming. Let's have the rest of the group meet back here in, say, ten minutes?"

Tension releases its stranglehold on the room as they all move quickly for the door. I sit numb, staring at the neatly bound jumble of words in front of me. "THESIS," the title page proclaims. What I really wanted was "ANTITHESIS." No, what I really wanted was to *perform* The Club in writing. The title page should say, "A PERFORM-ANCE." But that's not what it says. That's not what it is.

* * *

Sally touches my hand and nods as she moves toward the door. I offer her a weak smile and blink hard to keep back the tears. I think of Sally's eyes, of words she spoke to me only a week ago. I was standing in a classroom. Sally's classroom. Eager eyes looked me up and down.

* * *

"Today Stacy is here to tell you about her thesis," Sally says to the students. "It's an ethnographic study that she's done some rather unconventional things with."

A woman with sun-soaked hair smiles at me from the front row. Sally turns to me. "Tell them about your experiences . . . about how you've experimented with writing."

I look at them, earnest graduate students, searching for answers I can't give. Their silence entreats me to speak.

"I'm studying women's music performances at a folk music club. . . . It's a nonprofit organization devoted to presenting all types of nonmainstream music. This project has allowed me to explore critical, feminist, postmodern, and performance studies ideas with regard to women's music performances."

I pause . . . deciding . . . then begin, "I wrote the text in a dramatic, impressionistic form, but it's more than experimenting with writing. In fact, I think I started this project, doing it the way that I did, for very selfish reasons."

The air in the room goes still. "I wanted to write something that was interesting. Creative. Fun. But none of these motivations had very much to do with the people I would meet or the things I would discover."

The students shift nervously in their seats. "Now, after the fact, I see that innovative writing is a powerful means for presenting critical, feminist, postmodern, performative ethnography."

"How is it powerful?" the sunny woman asks.

"Because the aim of alternative ethnography is to highlight the multivocal, contested, incomplete, and performative nature of the culture studied, with the ultimate goal of social change. To do this in writing almost *requires* breaking with so-called conventional scholarly writing practices because of a desire to write others' voices . . . a desire to question your own authority as an author *within* your own text . . . a desire to collaborate with those you study."

"So how did you discover this after the fact?" she persists.

"Because these interests—postmodern, feminist, performative— only became clear in doing the project. But it's just me here." I wave a thick block of pages at them. "Just my words. Yes, I worked to let the voices speak for themselves, to leave interpretation open, to point out the vicarious irony of the ethnographer's authority, the reader's role in making textual meaning, but I could have done more. This writing is narcissistic and useless unless it changes the members' lives. And I doubt it will."

"But you tried," she soothes.

"I tried for the wrong reasons. Experimental writing does not allow you to escape the commitments and problems of knowledge and power. In fact, it's dangerous . . . dangerous because people use writing to skirt these responsibilities, to hide from them."

"*Dangerous?*" Sally says. "How is it dangerous?"

"It's dangerous because it's seductive!" I shout. "People like the *idea* of experimental writing. It's fashionable. And *dangerous*."

I stop, gulp stale air. Failure embraces me, laughs at my hasty delight with my stories, my writing. I tear from the room, unable to face them.

*　　*　　*

The telephone rings, pulling my blurry gaze from the computer screen. I stand, shaky, and reach for the receiver. "Hello?"

"Stacy, it's Sally. I just wanted to make sure you were OK. You left in such a hurry yesterday."

"Oh, um. . . ."

"I had the class take a break, but you'd left before I could get outside to the parking lot."

"I'm fine."

"What happened?"

"I'm just struggling with all of this. I felt very uncomfortable in front of your students—my peers—talking as if I've done something extraordinary. In so many ways, I've failed."

"*How* have you failed?" Her serene voice reminds me why we're friends and why her opinion means so much to me.

"I wanted to say what words can't say. To help the reader feel a small piece of what I've felt there, listening to the music. But it's just a bunch of words. . . ."

"Stacy, the powerful thing about this work is the way the reader experiences the tensions you've perceived at The Club, in women's music . . . the struggle between breaking convention and accepting convention, resisting and reifying. Your struggle to produce a socially approved thesis—to earn your degree and become legitimate in the academy—is complicated by your need to produce something intellectually honest, creative, and provocative. Do you see how your struggle *is* the struggle of The Club? The struggle of women's music?"

"I'm not sure."

"The Club, women's music, the thesis—all intersect and collide in what you've written. In some ways your work is like a kaleidoscope."

"A kaleidoscope," I murmur, relishing the word.

Notes

1. Yvonna S. Lincoln, "The Making of a Constructivist: A Remembrance of Transformations Past," *The Paradigm Dialog*, ed. Egon C. Guba (Newbury Park, Calif.: Sage, 1990), 85.

2. Erica Jong, "Fruits and Vegetables," *Fruits and Vegetables* (New York: Holt, Rinehart and Winston, 1971), 4–5.

3. Virginia Woolf, *Orlando* (New York: Harcourt, Brace, 1928), 268.

4. Stephen Connor, *Postmodern Culture: An Introduction to Theories of the Contemporary* (Oxford: Basil Blackwell, 1989), 57. The author notes that simulacrum is Jean Baudrillard's term for postmodern culture—culture is "pure simulation," in which reality is "manufactured"; experiences attempt to be, and are perceived as, "more real than reality itself." Simulacrum produces not a state of unreality, but of "hyperreality."

5. David Altheide and John Johnson, "Criteria for Assessing Interpretive Validity in Qualitative Research," *Handbook of Qualitative Research*, ed. Norman K. Denzin and Yvonna S. Lincoln (Thousand Oaks, Calif.: Sage, 1994), 490. The authors assert that ethnographers must strive to "obtain the members' perspectives on the social reality of the observed setting." An important element of this work is "faithfully reporting" the multivocality of cultural life, taking care to show "where the author's voice is located in relation" to the voices of others.

6. Jerome Kirk and Marc L. Miller, *Reliability and Validity in Qualitative Research* (Beverly Hills, Calif.: Sage, 1986), 12. The authors note that qualitative research does have a commitment to objectivity, but that the nature of this commitment is pluralistic. They write, "Natural human vision is binocular, for seeing the same thing simultaneously from more than one perspective gives a fuller understanding of its depth."

7. Research and Graduate Studies, *The Guide to Graduate Studies: The Official CSUS Guide to Policies, Procedures, and Format*, 2d ed., (Sacramento: California State University, Sacramento, 1995), 41.

8. Woolf, 268.

9. Sheryl Perlmutter Bowen and Nancy Wyatt, eds., "Visions of Synthesis, Visions of Critique," *Transforming Visions: Feminist Critiques in Communication Studies* (Creskill, N.J.: Hampton, 1993), 2–4. The authors discuss the mission of feminist scholarship in communication.

10. Patti Lather, *Getting Smart: Feminist Research and Pedagogy With/in the Postmodern* (New York: Routledge, 1991), 21.

11. Lather, 27–30. The author comments on the intersection of feminism and postmodernism.

12. Johannes Fabian, *Power and Performance: Ethnographic Explorations Through Proverbial Wisdom and Theater in Shaba Zaire* (Madison, Wis.: University of Wisconsin Press, 1990), 259.

13. Stephen Tyler, "Post-Modern Ethnography: From Document of the Occult to Occult Document," *Writing Culture: The Poetics and Politics of Ethnography*, ed. James Clifford and George Marcus (Berkeley: University of California Press, 1986), 126.

14. Dwight Conquergood, "Ethnography, Rhetoric and Performance," *Quarterly Journal of Speech* 78.1 (1992): 84.

15. Tyler, 131–35.

16. Egon C. Guba, ed., "The Alternative Paradigm Dialog," *The Paradigm Dialog* (Newbury Park, Calif.: Sage, 1990), 20, 27. Here I'm contrasting Guba's conventional (positivist) paradigm of inquiry (belief in a single, objective reality; in the possibility of detached observation; and in empirical verification) with the constructivist paradigm (multiple, culturally constructed realities; creative interaction among researcher and participant; and a dialectic process of scholarship).

17. Ruth Behar, "Introduction: Out of Exile," *Women Writing Culture*, eds. Ruth Behar and Deborah Gordon (Berkeley: University of California Press, 1995), 14.

18. Tyler, 136.

19. Lincoln, 72.

20. Lincoln, 72. Lincoln and Guba label these states of being ontological, educative, catalytic, and tactical authenticity. Lincoln notes that these states of being relate both to levels of understanding and an enhanced ability of participants to take action during and after an inquiry.

21. Guba, 27. The author summarizes the constructivist belief system (paradigm).

22. Lather, "Fertile Obsession: Validity After Poststructuralism," *The Sociological Quarterly* 34.3 (1993): 676.

23. Lather, 677–83. The author discusses these four senses of validity in detail.

24. Richard A. Rogers, "Rhythm and the Performance of Organization," *Text and Performance Quarterly* 14 (1994): 230. The author discusses the differences between western rhythms (which are singular and unifying) and African rhythms (which are multiple and incomplete).

25. Laurel Richardson, "Writing: A Method of Inquiry," *Handbook of Qualitative Research,* 522. The author's concept of crystallization provides a metaphor and visualization of these "multiple truths." She writes, "Crystallization, without losing structure, deconstructs the traditional idea of 'validity' (we feel how there is no single truth, we see how texts validate themselves); and crystallization provides us with a deepened, complex, thoroughly partial, understanding of the topic. Paradoxically, we know more and doubt what we know."

26. Guba, 20. The author summarizes the "basic belief system (paradigm) of conventional (positivist) inquiry."

27. Lincoln, 85. Paraphrase of the author, who writes, "we have no models for scientific knowledge that account for nonhierarchic learning, and we may have to borrow from the poet, the artist, the madman, the mystic."

In dealing with the truth of life's fictions, the dividing line between fact and fiction is tested, and reality and text become one. Narrative, in its many storied, performance, and textual forms, is all that we have.

Norman K. Denzin, *Interpretive Ethnography*[1]

Write with your eyes like painters, with your ears like musicians, with your feet like dancers. . . . Find the muse within you. The voice that lies buried under you, dig it up.

Gloria Anzaldúa, "Speaking in Tongues"[2]

I kept wondering as I was reading how she would analyze her own work as a piece of women's music—a musical text.

Mitch Allen, publisher, AltaMira Press

8

Refrain, not Finale

"A KALEIDOSCOPE," I say quietly as I watch my committee, my friends, file back into the room. Reliability, Validity, and their transgressive cousins do not return.

"OK," Gerri says warmly. "We've talked about method and the guiding theory for your work . . . but we'd like to hear a bit more about the specific critical and feminist theoretical choices you made in writing the thesis."

"About cultural capital, persistence, feminist performance?" I ask, unsure.

Gerri nods. "Why don't you start by telling us about cultural capital."

I sigh, feeling theory weigh heavy on my body. "Cultural capital is . . . meanings and pleasures 'that validate social experience of the subordinate'."[3]

"Are the people involved with The Club subordinate?" she asks.

"They view themselves as members of non-mainstream society and their work at The Club as a contribution to 'counterculture'."

Bill issues a weak cough. "How do you know this?"

"They say they provide space for music that would otherwise go unheard by Bay Area audiences. This supports their interest in non-mainstream music—bluegrass, folk, Celtic . . . and in some cases, it validates their politics."

"Do they set out to resist dominant culture or is resistance a by-product of their musical interests?" Nick asks.

"Fiske says that in order to create cultural capital, people must have certain knowledge and competence—knowledge of the force and meaning of their actions, and competence that comes from *actively* working against the dominant culture in creating and using cultural texts."[4]

"Is that what's happening at The Club?" he persists.

"I think so. People describe their efforts as 'important.' They say The Club is 'one of the few places where the focus is on the music.' They are very much aware that what they're doing is resisting main-stream music—mainstream culture." Sally smiles, encouraging me to continue.

"Even more interesting is that The Club serves the interests of many subcultural groups . . . creates multiple cultural capit*als* and competen*cies*. Some people come to hear only bluegrass shows, while others focus on singer-songwriters or instrumentalists, which throws into conflict these diverse interests, competencies, and capitals."

"Why?" Gerri asks.

"Because the subcultural interests of individuals can't always be met. Conflict among cultural capitals causes conflict among mem-bers—over the political and social content of the music, the ethnicity and sexual preference of the performer, even the composition of the audience."

"Did you see this kind of conflict?"

"Yes. I saw it in disagreements over who should be booked. In people who are uncomfortable with—and complain bitterly about—the audiences who come to see certain performers. In management's struggle to balance staying afloat with musical, social, and political agendas."

My skin itches with frustration. I don't understand these ques-tions, or myself. So why am I answering them—when I've written that there aren't answers, only my understandings and the under- standings of others? "Just get it over with," I tell myself.

"While the idea of cultural capital was salient, it didn't really describe The Club's long-term survival within dominant culture. I looked for a way to understand not only members' resistance, but their adaption and accommodation as well. Cynthia Lont's ideas on organizational persistence seemed to fit."[5]

Gerri nods. "Tell us about that."

"Lont defines persistence as 'the process that produces tension between political goals and the need for profit' for the organization.[6] Maybe we should back up and define resistance?"

"Yes."

"Mary Ellen Brown offers a clear definition, so I'll read from her work." I search through my notes, gaining assurance as I find the quote I want. "The processes of resistance, she writes, are ways in which subcultural groups contest 'hegemonic, or dominant pres- sures, and consequently obtain pleasure from what the political, social, and/or cultural system offers, despite that system's contradic- tory position in their lives'."[7]

I look up. Nick nods for me to continue. "Persistence incorpo- rates both the ideas of resistance," I say, "and the pleasures and meanings of cultural capital. It also accounts for the *acquiescence* of these groups to dominant pressures. Persistence is a continual and complex web of tensions—within the organization, between the organization and the dominant culture, and within the dominant culture. The organization is pushed and pulled by these tensions, and yet it persists, though not always in the same form."

"This the case for The Club?" Bill asks.

"Seems to be. It's survived many social, political, and organiza- tional challenges. . . . I need to add that though Lont focuses on the struggle between a need for profit and a need to accomplish political goals, I think The Club struggles to balance *musical* goals—authen- ticity, skill, artistry—and economic viability as a nonprofit."[8]

"How do women's music and feminist performances fit with the resistance and persistence ideas?" Nick asks.

"I decided to focus on women's music because it didn't seem to coincide with the other music presented at The Club."

"Why not?"

"All other music there fell within some identifiable *musical* genre—bluegrass or country or blues. But women's music didn't. I'd never heard that term before, and I couldn't get a sense of what the music sounded like. So I asked people."

Gerri looks up from her notes. "What did they say?"

"Things like, 'It's about issues important to women' or 'It's a code word for lesbian music.' I began wondering how the music served women's interests and *which* women's interests."

"What did you learn?" Bill asks.

"I learned that women's music originated during the feminist and lesbian-feminist movements of the '70s . . . that the term women's music *did* serve as a way to identify listeners and musicians as lesbians. And also that women's music had strong 'political and social meaning' for its supporters."[9]

Bill's eyes widen. "How so?"

"Let me read you what Lont says about this: 'The individuals and groups that produced the music were a tangible example of the power of women organized apart from the dominant culture. . . . The lesbian-feminist movement was made visible in concert halls and coffeehouses'."[10]

*   *   *

"*Chicken*," a voice hisses in my head.

Who is it? Nick? Laurel? Carolyn? Art? "*What?*" I reply, taking the bait.

"This is disgusting," the voice says. I still don't recognize it.

"*What?*"

"Listening to you talk about persistence, women's music. Listening to you *scientize* it. It's much better the way you've written it. Why don't you just tell them to read the book?"

"Hey!" I shout. "They *have* read it. This has nothing to do with what I've written. This has to do with my graduating."

She sighs. I sigh. "It's a shame, really," we say together, and I realize the voice is my own.

*   *   *

"Stacy?" Gerri says, pulling me back into the room.

"Yes?"

"Will you tell us about women's music at The Club?"

"Sorry. . . . At first, I wasn't sure how to distinguish among women's performances—that is, I couldn't tell which were *women's music* shows and which weren't."

"Did that change?" Nick asks.

"Somewhat. All women performers sing of women's lives—about motherhood, careers, their relationships with their bodies, relationships with other women, men, children. The difference seems to be in the artist's *depiction* of women."

"Depiction?"

"Yeah, some sing of weak, dependent women traditionally depicted in popular music, while others describe strong, loyal, tender, independent—and yes, feminist women—women who are equal partners in all areas of their lives."[11]

"Women's music features a stronger woman?" Bill asks.

"Based on my experience. But it's more complex than that."

"How?"

"It's tied up in the performance . . . in the interaction among performer, music, and audience. It's more than simply the content of the music."

"Enter your interest in performance theory," Nick says.

"Right. I started asking questions about performance as a way to understand the process—the *act* of persistence and resistance."

"Why performance?" he persists. "I'm not clear on the connection."

"Conquergood describes the efficacy of performance for understanding power and resistance." My finger finds his words, reverently bracketed on the page. "He says, 'Because it is public, performance is a site of struggle where competing interests intersect, and different viewpoints get articulated'."[12]

"So you focused on the struggle of women in performance?"

"Yes, and I became interested in how feminism intersects with performance theory."

"All new theoretical territory for you."

"I had a hard time because I felt I wasn't fully understanding anything—feminism, performance, or the feminist aesthetics of performance."

I pause and look at Nick, Gerri, and Bill. They return my gaze, stoic. I want to talk about how haphazard this all seems—picking and choosing what to read based on serendipitous discoveries in packed bibliographies. I know my work could have taken a very different turn had I not picked up this book on feminism or that article on women's music festivals. Their silence tells me to turn back.

"Langellier, Carter, and Hantzis adopt a feminist perspective in their discussion of 'embodiment' in performance . . . the emphasis it places on the 'body-act' of the performer—what the performer *does*—rather than his or her 'body-fact'—who the performer *is*. Embodiment works to *normalize* a performative 'double standard'."[13]

Nick drums a pencil on the table. "Double standard?"

"They say a woman performer must either 'divide herself *against* herself by denying her own body-fact and performing as a man . . . or she is defined as a marginal, female voice within the dominant paradigm'.[14] When women perform women's voices, they do so within not only this 'compulsory male' environment, but also within a 'compulsory heterosexual' context."[15]

"How is compulsory maleness and heterosexuality depicted in performance?" he asks.

"It's *constructed* within our cultural system of meanings. . . . It is always a 'doing,' as Butler suggests, so that gender identities are not inherent characteristics, but are created in performance. Gender is a body *act*, rather than a body *fact*."[16]

Nick nods, punctuating my words. "How is gender identity constructed in women's music performances?"

"Women's music problematizes the relationships between gender identity and gender performance[17] . . . So the performative double standard doubles back on itself."

"Doubles back?"

"It is created *and* questioned. Women's music performances simultaneously reify and make trouble for male and especially heterosexual assumptions about gender."

"How do they make trouble?"

"They embody and question the tensions between dominant culture and a feminist view of culture."

Bill pulls at his beard. "How is this played out in performances?"

"In voices and bodies." His eyebrows stretch upward, beckoning me to explain. "In the performer's lyrics and movement. In the audience's and employee's verbal and nonverbal communication with performers and each other, in my interactions and experiences."

"You quote Lather's idea that postmodern feminism questions not only the role of gender, but also race and sexual preference in oppression based in difference," Nick says. "How is race questioned in these performances?"

"Race and class are certainly issues for The Club—some members are very concerned about the overwhelmingly middle-class, white population on stage and in the audience. This is certainly true of women's music performances there—and women's music in general. In fact, in their study of women's music festivals, Eder, Staggenborg, and Sudderth take up this very issue, arguing that in striving to create a positive collective identity for lesbians, women's music in general and women's music festivals in particular make it difficult to reach out to women with diverse racial, class, and sexual identities[18] . . . And while racial and class diversity are organizational issues, I don't think they're being problematized—questioned or resisted—in these performances. The *absence* of women of color and women from different economic realities in women's music performances signifies a larger cultural lack."

"How so?" Gerri asks.

"These absences embody the organization . . . the music subculture . . . the dominant culture.

I look up and wait for a response. Nick nods and says, "Thanks. Now we'd like to talk about your writing choices. . . ."

"Before we do," I interrupt, "I'd also like to point out the salience of the kaleidoscope metaphor Marilyn Frye uses to describe feminism.[19] These performances are *kaleidoscopic*. They are the creative and ever-changing shapes, patterns, structures, silences . . . of gender, race, sexuality, music, organization, and culture."

Nick grins. "How do you write a kaleidoscope?"

"You write little notes," I say, smiling. "Little kaleidoscope notes."

*　　*　　*

"You wear the crisis of representation, the problem of writing the other,[20] like a party gown," the internal voice accuses. "Typing away in the safety of your little office. Not bothering to check with them."

"I *have* checked with them," I counter, defending my choices to myself. "I've talked to Sharon. And Mitchell and Brian. I tried to write a collective story."

"What's a collective story?" Sharon asks, invading my thoughts.

"Um, well, that's Laurel's term," I offer weakly.

"Laurel?" Sharon challenges.

"Sorry. Laurel Richardson, a sociologist who's written a lot about qualitative writing and . . ."

"A collective story is one in which you simultaneously give participants voice to speak of and for themselves and in which you, as a social analyst, speak of and for them,"[21] Laurel's voice says, joining in my internal play of words, defenses.

"Hmm," Sharon considers. "I think that's what you've done, although . . ."

"What?" I say too quickly, cutting her off.

"I think you stay too far away in the writing," she says. "I recognize myself, and Mitchell and Brian. I hear our voices—filtered through your words. But I don't hear much of *you*."

"That's why I wrote in the first person," I protest. "I didn't want to distance myself from you, didn't want to be the dispassionate observer, the omniscient narrator. I wanted us all to exist in the same time."[22]

"You bring us news of Sharon the manager and Sharon the person," Laurel says.[23] "Of Lina the performer and Lina the mother. Of Lucy the musician and Lucy the sister. All we get of you is Stacy the ethnographer."

"I *wanted* to write about Stacy the ethnographer."

"Don't you see?" Sharon asks. "To hide the other, more personal, parts of yourself is to distance yourself through your power as an author. To misrepresent yourself—and us—in the process."

"Laurel," I say, uncertain, desperate. "You told me writing is always partial. That the self is always present, and always repressed."

"Yes."

"That in writing, 'there's no getting it right, only getting it differently contoured and nuanced'."[24]

"How does the absence of your self change the contour, the nuance of your story?" she asks.

I wilt. "It makes me selfish, willing to reveal so much about the others . . . and so little of myself."

"And why am *I*—why are Sharon and Nick and Carolyn and Art and Lina and Cheryl—present in the text?" Laurel asks. "What kind of 'other' do we create to help *us* create?"

*   *   *

"Do you think you've written a postmodern, feminist ethnography?" Nick asks, startling me out of my reverie.

"Well, yes and no." My committee members wait for me to explain.

"That's what I've tried to write, to open the possibility for multiple interpretations, to challenge my understanding and create other partial glimpses. I think I've made room for multiple voices—women's voices, mostly—in a text shaped and coaxed and spoken and written by men."

"There are so many *men* in this text," I hear Laurel say in my head. "I want you to comment on why there are so many *men* in this text. Use that nice, high theory you have in your fieldnotes."

"Tell us more about that," Gerri says as if she's heard Laurel's words.

"OK," I begin. "Just as women's music performances are staged by and through The Club—an organization run, primarily, by men—my work highlights the voices of women—founders, artists, members, even theorists—within and through a text dominated by men."

"Such as . . ." Nick says.

"Well, you and Bill. Mitchell, Brian, and Ricky at The Club. Dwight and Stephen and other theorists. And, like women's music performances, this text at once reifies and makes trouble for male and heterosexual assumptions about gender."

"How so?" Bill asks.

"First let me say something about reading and performance."

"Sure."

"Texts are performances that are experienced, in still other performances, by readers. Like the assumed maleness and heterosexuality of performance, Donna Nudd writes of 'androcentric' reading strategies that teach readers to 'think as men, to identify with a male point of view, and to accept as normal and legitimate a male system of values'.[25] In the performative event of reading, gender perceptions are socially constructed."

"How does your text reify patriarchal and heterosexual gender assumptions?" Nick asks.

"I disciplined my writing, my self and the selves of the women in this text based on a male point of view, male values, male expectations." I look at Nick. "*Your* point of view, for instance. Your expectations. And Mitchell's. And Brian's." Nick nods, the bill of his baseball cap obscuring his eyes. I decide to continue.

"Like the women in my stories who police and discipline their bodies, I disciplined my text. I was constantly aware of the work's ability to measure up, to conform to a culturally constructed norm of a tight, controlled text, unfettered by emotion, weakness. At the same time, I couldn't have created this narrative without you, without these expectations."

"And how does your text resist a male reading position?" he presses.

"By asking readers to experience and to know this text in ways that move outside of dominant discourses. By featuring the voices of women. Like women's music, this text highlights my voice and the voices of Cheryl and Lina and Patty, Virginia and Sharon, Laurel and Judith as they are performed within the text and context." I stop, then add, "By writing for a feminist reader."

"I consider myself a feminist," Nick counters.

"Fair enough," I say. "I wrote for those who would identify with the female characters and characteristics of the text."

"As a man, can I make such identifications?" he asks, adjusting his cap.

"Nick, I think we agree that gender is not a biological, body fact. It is a performative act. *I* perform and constrain my work based on my construction of you, the male reader. But that doesn't mean *your* reading of this work isn't feminist. It may be feminist, masculinist, or both." Nick nods.

"For me," I continue, "the power in this work lies in the performative act of writing. Through my performance as a writer, women's bodies, selves, and identities are inscribed, marked, *and* set free, defying characterization. When read, they become and resist a 'linguistic flesh'."[26]

* * *

"A linguistic flesh." As I say this, my conversation with Sally a few days ago echoes in my mind.

"Sorry I'm late," Sally says as she glides into the seat across from me.

"Do you have time for coffee?"

"I have a student coming by in a few minutes." She offers me a sheaf of worn pages held together by a mottled rubber band. "I don't really have anything of intelligence or utility to say, but it was a joy to read."

I stare at my hands.

"Really." Her silence pulls my eyes to hers. "Gerri and Nick have invited me to the defense, but because I'm not officially a member of your committee, I don't feel comfortable participating."

"I understand."

"But I'll be there for support."

"Thanks. I appreciate all the time. . . ."

"I learned a lot."

This makes me laugh. What could I possibly teach my teacher? I smile up at her.

"Are you ready?"

"Technically. But it doesn't feel finished."

"The thesis is done. But the writing, the story, may be far from over."

"Maybe that's it. Sally, I feel like clutching it to me. I'm not ready to give it up."

Sally nods. "Trinh Minh-ha says 'to write is to become'.[27] I've got to run."

"Bye. Thanks again." I watch her walk away, then turn my eyes to the pages in front of me, to her words.

Stacy: A powerful and provocative piece of work. I'm led, by this, to consider so many issues, not the least of which is the question: What is scholarship in a postmodern world? Every time I raise a question about this work, this way of writing, the question gets thrown into play, which is, I think, part of the point. For example, I want to ask how we are to distinguish what are the ethnographer's "factual" observations and what is "fiction"? But as soon as I ask that, the references to postmodernism and the self-reflexivity and self-questioning in the piece remind me of the blur between fact and fiction in any ethnography. I recognize that this postmodern narrative perhaps needs to blur those lines to represent The Club, women's music, and your experience of these things.

"What *is* my experience of these things?" I ask aloud. "What have I become?" I stare at the napkin under my coffee until my eyes burn. I search my pockets for a pen and begin to write.

When I listen to music
I hear the words first.
Sound and rhythm
    Seep in much later.
Mind makes body wait.
What blood and muscle and bone,
Last to know,
    Already understand.

Is this text a song,
A made rhythm of words,
Sounding thoughts,
    Reaches my voice can't go?
Music beckons in type,
Plays in silences. Spaces. Endings.
Words unwritten
    Until read.

Fieldnotes, theory, defenses,
Words to prove me worthy,
Hear these first:
    Ethnographer, scholar, master.
Then in quiet verses,
Silences. Spaces. Endings.
Women, music I might become
    In words.

The flutter of verse,
Heat and rush of little notes,
Compose a second skin,
    A linguistic flesh.
Play it from within
Hear voices in keystrokes
The only music
    I know how to make.

*   *   *

"We'd like to hear your thoughts on how you've contributed to the work currently being done in ethnography," Gerri says. I stare at her, trying to shake off the memory. She places her hand on my thesis, pages and pages of words. "What's new or innovative here?"

I sigh. "Well, as Nick has said before, writers like Ellis and Bochner, Richardson, and Lather have laid the methodological groundwork for this kind of writing, and therefore what we need are more examples of alternative ethnographies, not more arguments." Nick nods. "But beyond creating an example, I really tried to write the ways performances create possibilities for resistance and change, as well as acquiescence. I worked to make what I wrote an experience of both The Club and women's music. I also wanted it to be an experience of method and theory."

"An *experience* of method and theory?" Nick asks.

"To make these things come alive for myself and the reader. For example, I think I've been persistent and performative in my writing."

Bill looks up. "Persistent?"

"Persistence not only helps me theoretically understand the organization and women's music performances there, but understand the very process of creating scholarship as well."

"How so?"

"By engaging persistence theory *and* creating persistent writing through . . . an impressionist tale, a poetic representation, a . . ."

Bill spreads his hands out on the table, examines his fingers. "Impressionist tale? Poetic representation?"

"Categories created by John Van Maanen and Laurel Richardson, scholars who endorse experimental ethnographic writing styles."

"Talk a bit about that," Gerri says.

I breathe in sharply, wanting to turn back. More categories, more words where there should be rhythm, sound, poetry. Theory fills my mouth instead. "I wrote what Van Maanen calls an impressionist tale, a 'vivid, novel-like account of fieldwork'.[28] I used literary techniques to tell stories about myself, the organization, and performances through the experiences of the characters."

"How is it a poetic representation?" Gerri asks.

"I also wrote songs and poetry. This was especially important because poetry and lyric allow silences and rhythms that other prose forms do not capture. Richardson says poetic writing 'engages the reader's (and listener's) bodies'. They can't resist."[29]

Nick opens his mouth to speak and our eyes turn to meet his. "Doesn't Richardson say poetic representations help problematize issues of legitimation—issues of reliability, validity, and truth?"[30]

I exhale. "Yes. And Faye Harrison says alternative writing forms encode 'truth claims—and alternative modes of theorizing—in a rhetoric of imagination.' It's writing that resists 'constructs of validity and reliability that privilege elitist, white male representations and explanations of the world'."[31]

Nick nods.

"My impressionist stories and poetic prose more closely align with Validity and Reliability's cousins—that is, assume their poststructuralist poses—and work toward the goals of feminist ethnography."

"How are they persistent?" Bill asks.

"They resist the kind of work the Methodology brothers advocate in both form and function. And yet my participation in this meeting means I hope this work still counts for scholarship within their paradigm. I guess time will tell whether I'm resistant or persistent. I hope I'm both."

Laughter erupts in the room, easing the tension. I press on. "I'd like to say something more about writing. In addition to being persistent, postmodern, and feminist—if that's what I've done—I wanted above all to be performative."

Gerri's eyebrows lift, speaking before she does. "Performative?"

"I wanted to *perform* the culture—perform women's music—in my writing. Conquergood calls for a 'performative cultural politics' where ethnographers actively reveal and question the tacit understandings of culture, the dynamics of oppression and resistance, and the knowledge on which we base these understandings.[32] That's what I tried to do . . . *embody* performance theory by writing a performative ethnography."

"Can you explain what you mean?" Bill asks.

"I wanted to create a print ethnography sensitive not only to the nuances of the performances I experienced, but also to the efficacy of a performative *presence*. Evocative, open. A *live* experience."[33]

"I'm still not clear. . . ."

"Maybe I need to say a bit about performance ethnography, work written to be staged and interpreted by performers. . . ."

"Sure," Bill says.

I search my notes on performance. "Here it is. Norm Denzin says the goal of performance ethnography is to 'create texts that produce a sudden awakening on the part of the viewer, who as audience member is also a performer.' The performed text is 'ever changing.' It constantly works against textual strategies that 'allow readers and listeners to assimilate the performance as a realist text.' "[34]

Bill nods, beckoning me to continue. "I wanted to write a narrative that not only reveals me as an actor, but engages readers as performers. A story that moves and transforms itself. A text that resists assimilation and categorization."

"Like your experiences at The Club?" Gerri asks.

"*Yes*," I say, seeing this clearly now. "Denzin says that the move to performance ethnography is something new, a blurring of the boundaries between scholarly texts and performance. But he cautions performance ethnographers to create texts that are 'accessible and performable'."[35]

"And you've created such a text?" Nick asks.

"I tried to make a text that 'privileges experience,' that 'reawakens and recovers' the reader's 'capacity to participate and feel too'."[36]

Nick shakes his head. "Why not perform it, then?"

$$* \quad * \quad *$$

Scene Eight

Stacy, the committee members, and the onlookers are sitting at the conference room table. Stacy slumps in her chair across from them. Nick, Bill, and Gerri exchange a knowing glance. Bill nods.

BILL: OK. We have just one more question.

STACY: Yes?

BILL: What is the practical relevance of this project? How can the organization members *use* what you've written?

[*A white spotlight shines on Stacy. She shields her eyes.*]

BILL: Stacy?

STACY: Yes.

BILL: How have you helped the members?

STACY: I haven't. Not yet.

NICK: You haven't helped them? Isn't that the goal of critical and feminist scholarship?

STACY: Yes, but. . . .

GERRI: But what?

STACY: But I will help them. They trust me. We've been talking about my writing a book about the organization. Something they could sell as a sort of biography or organizational history. . . .

BILL: So what you've done has no practical application?

STACY: How can it? I didn't write it for them. I wrote it for me! I wrote it for you!

[*Stacy stands and faces the audience.*]

STACY: I wrote it for me! I wrote it for you!

[*She collapses on the floor, sobbing.*]

*   *   *

"OK, stop there," I say, turning my back on the performers and moving to the edge of the stage.

"This scene is missing something. Maybe we should have Sharon and Laurel come in before she speaks to the audience?" I search the seats before me, impatient for a response.

"You're directing this one," Sharon says. I peer into the empty auditorium, search for the fuzzy outlines of her hair.

"I know . . . but I'd like your input. Maybe we should do it like the performance in Scene Six, with everybody on stage? What do you think?"

"Too much," Bill says from behind me.

"One of those tawdry finale endings," Reliability scoffs from the front row.

"You'd expect some big musical number," Validity adds. He plunges an elbow into his brother's side.

"Maybe you're right. I don't know. . . ."

From across the aisle, Rhizomatic scowls. "Go with your instincts."

Paralogical nods. "I like the abrupt ending. Just leave 'em hanging."

"Ah, yes," Voluptuous says.

"Yuck!" Nick's voice booms over the sound system. "I think it's a terrible ending."

Laurel, Carolyn, and Art step from the shadows of the stage. "You're doing a monologue. . . ." Art says.

"Where are the voices of the text?" Laurel asks. "We need to hear the voices of the performers. The members. The committee. We need to hear your voice. And the voice of theory."

"More light and sound," Carolyn suggests. "More music. More *emotion.*"

"Let's do a kaleidoscope ending," I suggest.

*   *   *

Scene Eight

Stacy, the committee members, and the onlookers are sitting at the conference room table, stage right. Stacy slumps in her chair across from them. Nick, Bill, and Gerri exchange a knowing glance. Bill nods.

BILL: OK. We have just one more question.

STACY: Yes?

BILL: What is the practical relevance of this project? How can the organization members *use* what you've written?

[*A red spotlight shines on Stacy. She shields her eyes.*]

BILL: Stacy?

STACY: Yes.

BILL: How have you helped the members?

STACY: I haven't. Not yet.

NICK: You haven't helped them? Isn't that the goal of critical and feminist scholarship?

STACY: Yes, but. . . .

GERRI: But what?

STACY: But I will help them. They trust me. We've been talking about my writing a book about the organization. Something they could sell as a sort of biography or organizational history. . . .

BILL: So what you've done has no practical application?

STACY: How can it? I didn't write it for them. I wrote it for me! I wrote it for you!

[*Stacy stands and faces the audience.*]

STACY: I wrote it for me! I wrote it for you!

[*Three short knocks are heard from the darkness at stage left. The red spot dims and a yellow spot shines on Reliability and Validity, who sit stiffly behind a large, old-fashioned desk. Brian sits across from them, elbows on the desk and face buried in his hands. Reliability pounds on the desk with his fist twice more.*]

RELIABILITY: How many Asians do you employ?

BRIAN: I don't know.

VALIDITY: How many Blacks? How many gay and lesbian performers?

BRIAN: I don't know. I don't ask those questions.

RELIABILITY: How do you expect us to evaluate this operation? To give your efforts currency? Unless you show proof of the Truth and consistency of the organization, we cannot approve.

BRIAN: I'm not so sure I want your approval.

[*The yellow spot fades. A blue spotlight illuminates Rhizomatic at center stage. He nods and begins to play a drum strapped across his chest. Lina, Cheryl, Patty, and Lucy move center stage with their guitars and circle Rhizomatic. They begin playing various accompaniments. Lina begins humming.*]

LINA: [*Singing*] There are days when every bone in her body is achin'. When she feels like everyone hates her. And she cannot speak.

PATTY: [*Singing*] My God, all the things I did to you. You were my enemy, never my friend.

[*Sharon, Virginia, Paralogical, and Voluptuous join the activity at center stage. Sharon sways to the music. Virginia and Voluptuous embrace, begin a waltz. Paralogical dances wildly, her body punctuating a rhythm out of synch with the beat. Stacy cautiously approaches and watches the dancers. She scribbles furiously in a tiny notebook, then stops to watch the dancers once more. After several moments, she throws the notebook to the floor and begins swaying to the music.*]

PATTY: [*Singing*] My body, my friend, forgive me if you can.

LUCY: [*Singing*] Don't you know how much you have to give?

CHERYL: [*Singing*] Are you more amazed at how things change? Or how they stay the same?

LINA: [*Singing*] Don't it make you want to cry?

[*Red lights slowly illuminate the conference room scene at stage right. Bill, Gerri, and Nick talk silently among themselves. Yellow lights come up on the organization scene at stage left. Reliability, Validity, and Brian continue to argue silently. The music softens. Sharon, Virginia, Voluptuous, and Paralogical continue to dance. Ironic moves center stage and takes Stacy's hand. Laurel joins them. The three move downstage, toward the audience. A white spotlight shines on them. Stacy speaks to the audience and Ironic moves his hands in cryptic sign language.*]

STACY: It was the music that brought me here. Writer, detective, woman struggling to pen the kaleidoscope play. To paint fleeting harmony, dizzy change. To stir milk's smooth surface. To verse tide pools of resistance, eddies of persistence. Learn to love.

LAUREL: Learn to know more and doubt that.

STACY: To know more and doubt that.

[*The stage lights flash twice, then go out.*]

Notes

1. Norman K. Denzin, *Interpretive Ethnography: Ethnographic Practices for the 21st Century* (Thousand Oaks, Calif.: Sage, 1997), 266.
2. Gloria Anzaldúa, "Speaking in Tongues: A Letter to Third World Women Writers," *This Bridge Called My Back: Writings By Radical Women of Color*, 2d ed., eds. Cherríe Moraga and Gloria Anzaldúa (New York: Kitchen Table, 1983), 173.
3. John Fiske, *Television Culture* (London: Routledge, 1987), 19.
4. Fiske, 19. These knowledges and competencies are a source of power for subcultural actors. The author notes, "there is a power in maintaining one's social identity in opposition to that proposed by the dominant ideology, there is a power in asserting one's own subcultural values against the dominant ones. There is, in short, a power in being different."
5. Cynthia Lont, "Subcultural Persistence: The Case of Redwood Records," *Women's Studies in Communication* 11 (Spring 1988): 50–60. See also Lont's "Persistence of Subcultural Organizations: An Analysis Surrounding the Process of Organizational Change," *Communication Quarterly* 38.1 (1990) and "Between Rock and a Hard Place: A Model of Subcultural Persistence and Women's Music," diss., University of Iowa, 1984.
6. Lont, "Subcultural Persistence," 51.
7. Mary Ellen Brown, "Introduction," *Television and Women's Culture: The Politics of the Popular* (London: Sage, 1990), 12.
8. Lont, "Subcultural Persistence," 50.
9. Lont, "Women's Music: No Longer a Small Private Party," *Rockin' the Boat: Mass Music and Mass Movements*, ed. Reebee Garofalo (Boston: South End Press, 1992), 240–42.
10. Lont, "Women's Music," 242.
11. Lont, "Between Rock and a Hard Place," 94. From Lont's description of the women in women's music.
12. Dwight Conquergood, "Poetics, Play, Process, and Power: The Performative Turn in Anthropology," *Text and Performance Quarterly* 9 (1989): 84.
13. Kristin M. Langellier, Kathryn Carter, and Darlene Hantzis, "Performing Differences: Feminism and Performance Studies," *Transforming Visions: Feminist Critiques in Communication Studies*, ed. Sheryl Perlmutter Bowen and Nancy Wyatt (Creskell, N.J.: Hampton Press, 1993), 91–92.
14. Langellier, Carter, and Hantzis, 93.

15. Langellier, Carter, and Hantzis, 94.
16. Langellier, Carter, and Hantzis, 93. The authors note that "Body-fact addresses sex as an attribute of the individual, but obscures gender as the social and cultural system of power relations in which performance is situated. Body-act privileges male voices and interests and masks its gender politics."
17. Judith Butler, *Gender Trouble* (New York: Routledge, 1990), 137.
18. Donna Eder, Suzanne Staggenborg, and Lori Sudderth, "The National Women's Music Festival: Collective Identity and Diversity in a Lesbian-Feminist Community," *Journal of Contemporary Ethnography* 23.4 (1995): 511. The authors note that in striving to create a positive collective identity for lesbians, women's music in general and women's music festivals in particular make it difficult to reach out to culturally and racially diverse groups of women. See also "Women's Culture and Social Change: Evidence from the National Women's Music Festival" by Staggenborg, Eder, and Sudderth.
19. Marilyn Frye, *The Politics of Reality: Essays in Feminist Theory* (New York: Crossing Press, 1983), 259. The author characterizes feminism as kaleidoscopic: "something whose shapes, structures and patterns alter with every turn of feminist creativity." ·
20. Laurel Richardson, "The Collective Story: Postmodernism and the Writing of Sociology," *Sociological Focus* 21.3 (1988): 200. The author describes the crisis of representation as "uncertainty about what constitutes adequate depiction of social reality."
21. Richardson, "The Collective Story," 204. The collective story involves listening to the personal stories of cultural members and placing these narratives within the larger social and historical context, with an eye to discerning the elements of contemporary culture that are disempowering to these members.
22. Conquergood, "Ethnography, Rhetoric and Performance," *Quarterly Journal of Speech* 78.1 (1992): 85. The author urges ethnographers, in their writing practices as well as their fieldwork, to "keep experimenting with ways to meet the Other on the same ground, in the same Time."
23. Raymond Carver, "On Writing," *Fires* (New York: Vintage Books, 1984), 15. Short story writer and poet Raymond Carver writes that good fiction should bring us the "news of the world."
24. Richardson, "Writing: A Method of Inquiry," *Handbook of Qualitative Research*, ed. Norman K. Denzin and Yvonna S. Lincoln (Thousank Oaks, Calif.: Sage, 1994), 520–21.

25. Donna Marie Nudd, "Establishing the Balance: Re-examining Students' Androcentric Readings of Katherine Anne Porter's 'Rope'," *Communication Education* 40 (1991): 49.
26. Trinh T. Minh-ha, *Woman, Native, Other: Writing Postcoloniality and Feminism* (Bloomington: Indiana University Press, 1989), 38. The author notes that women's writing is of and through the body. This writing "becomes 'organic writing,' 'nurturing writing' (nouricriture), resisting separation. It becomes a 'connoting material,' a 'kneading dough,' a 'linguistic flesh.'"
27. Minh-ha, 18.
28. John Van Maanen, *Tales of the Field* (Chicago: University of Chicago Press, 1988), 104–105.
29. Richardson, "Writing: A Method of Inquiry," 522.
30. Richardson, "Writing: A Method of Inquiry," 522. The author notes the constructedness of all texts; therefore, "poetry helps problematize reliability, validity, and truth."
31. Faye V. Harrison, "Writing Against the Grain: Cultural Politics of Difference in the Work of Alice Walker," *Women Writing Culture*, eds. Ruth Behar and Deborah Gordon (Berkeley: University of California Press, 1995), 234.
32. Conquergood, "Ethnography, Rhetoric and Performance," 95.
33. Marianne Paget, "Performing the Text," *Representation in Ethnography*, ed. John Van Maanen (Thousand Oaks, Calif.: Sage, 1995), 228. The author writes that "Performance permits a live experience," a "vivid present of watching and hearing . . ."
34. Denzin, 116.
35. Denzin, 123.
36. Paget, 240.

Works Cited

Abbate, Carolyn. "Opera; or the Envoicing of Women." *Musicology and Difference: Gender and Sexuality in Music Scholarship.* Ed. Ruth A. Solie. Berkeley: University of California Press, 1993. 225–58.

Altheide, David L., and John M. Johnson. "Criteria for Assessing Interpretive Validity in Qualitative Research." *Handbook of Qualitative Research.* Ed. Norman K. Denzin and Yvonna S. Lincoln. Thousand Oaks, Calif.: Sage, 1994. 485–99.

Anzaldúa, Gloria. "Speaking in Tongues: A Letter to Third World Women Writers." *This Bridge Called My Back: Writings by Radical Women of Color.* 2d ed. Ed. Cherríe Moraga and Gloria Anzaldúa. New York: Kitchen Table, Women of Color Press, 1983. 165–74.

Bauman, Richard. *Verbal Art as Performance.* Prospect Heights, Ill.: Waveland, 1984.

Bayton, Mavis. "Feminist Musical Practice: Problems and Contradictions." *Rock and Popular Music: Politics, Policies, Institutions.* Ed. Tony Bennett, Simon Frith, Lawrence Grossberg, John Shepherd, and Graeme Turner. London: Routledge, 1993. 177–92.

Behar, Ruth. "Introduction: Out of Exile." *Women Writing Culture.* Ed. Ruth Behar and Deborah Gordon. Berkeley: University of California Press, 1995. 1–32.

Bell, Elizabeth. "Toward a Pleasure-Centered Economy: Wondering a Feminist Aesthetics of Performance." *Text and Performance Quarterly* 15.2 (1995): 99–121.

Blair, Carole, Marsha S. Jeppeson, and Enrico Pucci, Jr. "Public Memorializing in Postmodernity: The Vietnam Veterans Memorial as Prototype." *Critical Questions: Invention, Creativity and the Criticism of Discourse and Media.* Ed. William L. Nothstine, Carole Blair, and Gary A. Copeland. New York: St. Martin's Press, 1994. 350–82.

Block, Rory. "Joliet Bound." *When a Woman Gets the Blues.* Rounder, 1995.

———. "Ain't I A Woman." *Ain't I A Woman.* Rounder, 1992.

———. "Road To Mexico." *Ain't I A Woman.* Rounder, 1992.

————. "Mama's Blues." *Mama's Blues*. Rounder, 1991.

Bochner, Arthur P., and Carolyn Ellis. "Talking Over Ethnography." *Composing Ethnography: Alternative Forms of Qualitative Writing*. Ed. Carolyn Ellis and Arthur P. Bochner. Walnut Creek, Calif.: AltaMira Press, 1996. 13–45.

Bordo, Susan. *Unbearable Weight: Feminism, Western Culture, and the Body*. Berkeley: University of California Press, 1993.

Brislin, Kate, and Katy Moffatt. *Sleepless Nights*. Rounder, 1996.

Brown, Mary Ellen. "Introduction." *Television and Women's Culture: The Politics of the Popular*. Ed. Mary Ellen Brown. London: Sage, 1990. 11–22.

Burke, Kenneth. *A Rhetoric of Motives*. Berkeley: University of California Press, 1950.

Butler, Judith. *Bodies That Matter: On the Discursive Limits of "Sex."* New York: Routledge, 1993.

————. *Gender Trouble: Feminism and the Subversion of Identity*. New York: Routledge, 1990.

Carver, Raymond. "On Writing." *Fires*. New York: Vintage Books, 1980.

Connor, Steven. *Postmodern Culture: An Introduction to Theories of the Contemporary*. Oxford: Basil Blackwell, 1989.

Conquergood, Dwight. "Ethnography, Rhetoric and Performance." *Quarterly Journal of Speech* 78.1 (1992): 80–97.

————. "Poetics, Play, Process, and Power: The Performative Turn in Anthropology." *Text and Performance Quarterly* 9 (1989): 82–88.

de Beauvoir, Simone. *All Said and Done*. London: Deutsch and Weidenfeld and Nicolson, 1974.

Denzin, Norman K. *Interpretive Ethnography: Ethnographic Practices for the 21st Century*. Thousand Oaks, Calif.: Sage, 1997.

Eder, Donna, Suzanne Staggenborg, and Lori Sudderth. "The National Women's Music Festival: Collective Identity and Diversity in a Lesbian-Feminist Community." *Journal of Contemporary Ethnography* 23.4 (1995): 485–515.

Engh, Barbara. "Loving It: Music and Criticism in Roland Barthes." *Musicology and Difference: Gender and Sexuality in Music Scholarship*. Ed. Ruth A. Solie. Berkeley: University of California Press, 1993. 66–79.

Fabian, Johannes. *Power and Performance: Ethnographic Explorations Through Proverbial Wisdom and Theater in Shaba Zaire.* Madison: University of Wisconsin Press, 1990.

Finn, Janet L. "Ella Cara Deloria and Mourning Dove: Writing for Cultures, Writing Against the Grain." *Women Writing Culture.* Ed. Ruth Behar and Deborah A. Gordon. Berkeley: University of California Press, 1995. 131–47.

Fiske, John. *Television Culture.* London: Routledge, 1987.

Fitzhenry, Robert I. *The Harper Book of Quotations.* 3d ed. New York: HarperCollins, 1993.

Flax, Jane. *Thinking Fragments: Psychoanalysis, Feminism, and Postmodernism in the Contemporary West.* Berkeley: University of California Press, 1990.

Foss, Sonja, Karen A. Foss, and Robert Trapp. "Kenneth Burke." *Contemporary Perspectives on Rhetoric.* Prospect Heights, Ill.: 1991. 169–208.

Foucault, Michel. "The Eye of Power." *Power/Knowledge.* Ed. and trans. C. Gordo. New York: Pantheon, 1977.

Frye, Marilyn. *The Politics of Reality: Essays in Feminist Theory.* New York: Crossing Press, 1983.

Gonzalez, M. Cristina. *The Four Seasons of Ethnography.* Unpublished manuscript, 1996.

Guba, Egon C. "The Alternative Paradigm Dialog." *The Paradigm Dialog.* Ed. Egon C. Guba. Newbury Park, Calif.: Sage, 1990. 17–27.

Harrison, Faye V. "Writing Against the Grain: Cultural Politics of Difference in the Work of Alice Walker." *Women Writing Culture.* Ed. Ruth Behar and Deborah A. Gordon. Berkeley: University of California Press, 1995. 233–45.

Hassan, Ihab. *The Dismemberment of Orpheus: Toward a Postmodern Literature.* New York: Oxford University Press, 1982.

hooks, bell. *Black Looks: Race and Representation.* Boston: South End Press, 1992.

———. *Ain't I a Woman: Black Women and Feminism.* Boston: South End Press, 1981.

Hunter, Anne Marie. "Numbering the Hairs of Our Heads: Male Social Control and the All-Seeing Male God." *Journal of Feminist Studies in Religion* 8.2 (1992): 7–23.

Hurston, Zora Neale. *Their Eyes Were Watching God*. 1937. Foreword Mary Helen Washington, Afterword Henry Louis Gates, Jr. San Bernardino, Calif.: Borgo, 1990.

Jong, Erica. "Fruits and Vegetables." *Fruits and Vegetables*. New York: Holt, Rinehart and Winston, 1971. 1–10.

Kirk, Jerome, and Marc L. Miller. *Reliability and Validity in Qualitative Research*. Beverly Hills, Calif.: Sage, 1986.

Langellier, Kristin M., Kathryn Carter, and Darlene Hantzis. "Performing Differences: Feminism and Performance Studies." *Transforming Visions: Feminist Critiques in Communication Studies*. Ed. Sheryl Perlmutter Bowen and Nancy Wyatt. Creskill, N.J.: Hampton Press, 1993. 87–124.

Lather, Patti. "Fertile Obsession: Validity After Poststructuralism." *Sociological Quarterly* 34.3 (1993): 673–93.

———. *Getting Smart: Feminist Research and Pedagogy with/in the Postmodern*. New York: Routledge, 1991.

Lincoln, Yvonna S. "The Making of a Constructivist: A Remembrance of Transformations Past." *The Paradigm Dialog*. Ed. Egon C. Guba. Newbury Park, Calif.: Sage, 1990. 67–87.

Lont, Cynthia M. "Women's Music: No Longer a Small Private Party." *Rockin' the Boat: Mass Music and Mass Movements*. Ed. Reebee Garofalo. Boston: South End Press, 1992. 241–54.

———. "Persistence of Subcultural Organizations: An Analysis Surrounding the Process of Subcultural Change." *Communication Quarterly* 38.1 (1990): 1–12.

———. "Subcultural Persistence: The Case of Redwood Records." *Women's Studies in Communication* 11 (spring 1988): 50–60.

———. "Between Rock and a Hard Place: A Model of Subcultural Persistence and Women's Music." Diss., University of Iowa, 1984.

McClary, Susan. "Same As It Ever Was: Youth Culture and Music." *Rock She Wrote: Women Write About Rock, Pop, and Rap*. Ed. Evelyn McDonnell and Ann Powers. New York: Delta, 1995. 440–54.

Mifflin, Margot. "The Fallacy of Feminism in Rock." *Rock She Wrote: Women Write About Rock, Pop, and Rap*. Ed. Evelyn McDonnell and Ann Powers. New York: Delta, 1995. 76–79.

Minh-ha, Trinh T. *Woman, Native, Other: Writing Postcoloniality and Feminism*. Bloomington, Ind.: Indiana University Press, 1989.

Mulvey, Laura. "Visual Pleasure and Narrative Cinema." *Art After Modernism: Rethinking Representation*. Ed. Brian Wallis. New York: New York Museum of Contemporary Art, 1984. 361–74.

Nietzsche, Friedrich. *The Gay Science; With a Prelude in Rhymes and an Appendix of Songs*. 1st ed. Trans. Walter Kaufmann. New York: Vintage Books, 1974.

Nudd, Donna Marie. "Establishing the Balance: Re-examining Students' Androcentric Readings of Katherine Anne Porter's 'Rope'." *Communication Education* 40 (1991): 49–59.

Paget, Marianne. "Performing the Text." *Representation in Ethnography*. Ed. John Van Maanen. Thousand Oaks, Calif.: Sage, 1995. 222–44.

Partnow, Elaine, ed. *The Quotable Woman: An Encyclopedia of Useful Quotations*. Vol. 1. Los Angeles: Pinnacle, 1977.

Petersen, Karen E. "An Investigation into Women-Identified Music in the United States." *Music and Women in Cross-Cultural Perspective*. Ed. Ellen Koskoff. New York: Greenwood, 1987. 203–12.

Perlmutter Bowen, Sheryl, and Nancy Wyatt, eds. "Visions of Synthesis, Visions of Critique." *Transforming Visions: Feminist Critiques in Communication Studies*. Creskill, N.J.: Hampton Press, 1993. 1–18.

Powers, Ann. "Who's That Girl?" *Rock She Wrote: Women Write About Rock, Pop, and Rap*. Ed. Evelyn McDonnell and Ann Powers. New York: Delta, 1995. 459–67.

Rajchman, John. "Postmodernism in a Nominalist Frame: The Emergence and Diffusion of a Cultural Category." *Flash Art* 137 (1987): 49–51.

Research and Graduate Studies. *Guide to Graduate Studies: The Official CSUS Guide to Policies, Procedures, and Format*. 2d ed. Sacramento: California State University, Sacramento, 1995.

Richardson, Laurel. "Writing: A Method of Inquiry." *Handbook of Qualitative Research*. Ed. Norman K. Denzin and Yvonna S. Lincoln. Thousand Oaks, Calif.: Sage, 1994. 516–29.

———. "Postmodern Social Theory: Representational Practices." *Sociological Theory* 9:2 (1991): 173–80.

———. "The Collective Story: Postmodernism and the Writing of Sociology." *Sociological Focus* 21.3 (1988): 199–208.

Robertson, Carol E. "Power and Gender in the Musical Experiences of Women." *Music and Women in Cross-Cultural Perspective.* Ed. Ellen Koskoff. New York: Greenwood, 1987. 225–44.

Rogers, Richard A. "Rhythm and the Performance of Organization." *Text and Performance Quarterly* 14 (1994): 222–37.

Rosenblatt, Louise M. "The Transactional Theory: Against Dualisms." *College English* 55.4 (1993): 377–86.

Rosaldo, Renato. *Culture and Truth: The Remaking of Social Analysis.* Boston: Beacon, 1993.

Seeger, Peggy. "Getting It Right." *Almost Commercially Viable, No Spring Chickens.* Peggy Seeger and Irene Scott. Golden Egg Productions, 1993.

———. "I'm Gonna Be an Engineer." *Peggy Seeger, The Folkways Years 1955–1992, Songs of Love and Politics.* Smithsonian/Folkways, 1992.

———. "Song of Myself." *Peggy Seeger, The Folkways Years 1955–1992, Songs of Love and Politics.* Smithsonian/Folkways, 1992.

Seidman, Steven. "Postmodern Anxiety: The Politics of Epistemology." *Sociological Theory* 9.2 (1991): 180–90.

Solie, Ruth A., ed. "Introduction: On 'Difference'." *Musicology and Difference: Gender and Sexuality in Music Scholarship.* Berkeley: University of California Press, 1993. 1–20.

Sorrells, Rosalie. Letter to Friends of the Freight. *Calendar.* Dec. 1995. Berkeley, Calif.: Berkeley Society for the Preservation of Traditional Music.

Staggenborg, Suzanne, Donna Eder, and Lori Sudderth. "Women's Culture and Social Change: Evidence for the National Women's Music Festival." *Berkeley Journal of Sociology* 38 (1993–94): 31–56.

Sutton, Terri. "Whatever Happened to 'Women's Music'?" *Utne Reader.* Jan./Feb. 1992: 30–34.

Tyler, Stephen A. "Post-Modern Ethnography: From Document of the Occult to Occult Document." *Writing Culture: The Poetics and Politics of Ethnography.* Ed. James Clifford and George Marcus. Berkeley: University of California Press, 1986. 122–40.

Van Maanen, John. *Tales of the Field.* Chicago: University of Chicago Press, 1988.

Vanden Heuvel, Michael. *Performing Drama/Dramatizing Performance: Alternative Theater and the Dramatic Text.* Ann Arbor: University of Michigan Press, 1994.

Wheeler, Cheryl. "Act of Nature." *Driving Home*. Philo, 1993.

———. "75 Septembers." *Driving Home*. Philo, 1993.

Woolf, Virginia. *Orlando: A Biography*. New York: Harcourt, Brace, 1928.

Yeats, William Butler. "Among School Children." *Collected Poems of W. B. Yeats*. New York: Macmillan, 1946. 251.

Index

About the Author

I SHARE MY BIRTHDAY with Mata Hari and was recently described (in an informal ethnographic survey, of course) by my colleagues as "caring," "diligent," and "spicy." I'm not sure whether these words are truth or fiction, but they'll do. Beyond these adjectives, I am a doctoral student in performance studies at The University of Texas at Austin, where I live with my husband. When I'm not (and sometimes when I am) listening to music, I try to make performances and ethnographies that are full of care and diligence and, of course, are a little bit spicy.